LITERATURE MADE EASY

WILLIAM SHAKESPEARE'S

A MIDSUMMER NIGHT'S DREAM

Written by **MICHAEL KERRIGAN**
WITH TONY BUZAN

BARRON'S

First edition for the United States and Canada published by Barron's
Educational Series, Inc., 1999

First published in the United Kingdom by Hodder & Stoughton Ltd.
under the title: *Teach Yourself Literature Guides: A Guide to A
Midsummer Night's Dream*

American text edited by Elizabeth Schmid

All inquiries should be addressed to:
Barron's Educational Series, Inc.
250 Wireless Boulevard
Hauppauge, New York 11788
http://www.barronseduc.com

International Standard Book No. 0-7641-0827-1

Library of Congress Catalog Card No. 98-74653

Printed in the United States of America
9 8 7 6 5 4 3 2 1

R0/74/43758

CONTENTS

Important Note to Students About Line References

Line references are to The New Folger Library edition of Shakespeare's *A Midsummer Night's Dream*. If you have another edition, the line numbers may vary slightly from those provided in this book, although the act and scene numbers should be the same. The line number references from the New Folger edition have been provided to help direct you to specific parts of the play, but often will not be an exact match for line numbers in other editions.

There are five important things you must know about your brain and memory to revolutionize the way you study:

◆ how your memory ("recall") works *while* you are learning
◆ how your memory works *after* you have finished learning
◆ how to use Mind Maps – a special technique for helping you with all aspects of your studies
◆ how to prepare for tests and exams.

Recall during learning
– THE NEED FOR BREAKS

When you are studying, your memory can concentrate, understand, and remember well for between 20 and 45 minutes at a time; then it needs a break. If you continue for longer than this without a break your memory starts to break down. If you study for hours nonstop, you will remember only a small fraction of what you have been trying to learn, and you will have wasted hours of valuable time.

So, ideally, *study for less than an hour*, then take a five- to ten-minute break. During the break listen to music, go for a walk, do some exercise, or just daydream. (Daydreaming is a necessary brain-power booster – geniuses do it regularly.) During the break your brain will be sorting out what it has been learning, and you will go back to your books with the new information safely stored and organized in your memory. We recommend breaks at regular intervals as you work through this book: Make sure you take them!

Recall after learning
— THE WAVES OF YOUR MEMORY

What do you think begins to happen to your memory right after you have finished learning something? Does it immediately start forgetting? No! Your brain actually *increases* its power and continues remembering. For a short time after your study session, your brain integrates the information, making a more complete picture of everything it has just learned. Only then does the rapid decline in memory begin, and as much as 80 percent of what you have learned can be forgotten in a day.

However, if you catch the top of the wave of your memory, and briefly review (look back over) what you have been studying at the right time, the memory is imprinted far more strongly, and stays at the crest of the wave for a much longer time. To maximize your brain's power to remember, take a few minutes at the end of a day and use a Mind Map to review what you have learned. Then review it at the end of a week, again at the end of a month, and finally a week before your test or exam. That way you'll ride your memory wave all the way there – and beyond!

The Mind Map®
— A PICTURE OF THE WAY YOU THINK

Do you like taking notes? More important, do you like having to go back over and learn them before tests or exams? Most students I know certainly do not! And how do you take your notes? Most people take notes on lined paper, using blue or black ink. The result, visually, is boring. And what does *your* brain do when it is bored? It turns off, tunes out, and goes to sleep! Add a dash of color, rhythm, imagination, and the whole note-taking process becomes much more fun, uses more of your brain's abilities, and improves your recall and understanding.

Generally, your Mind Map is highly personal and need not be understandable to any other person. It mirrors *your* brain. Its purpose is to build up your "memory muscle" by creating images that will help you recall instantly the most important points about the characters and plot sequences in a work of fiction you are studying.

You will find Mind Maps throughout this book. Study them, add some color, personalize them, and then try drawing your own – you'll remember them far better. Stick them in your files and on your walls for a quick-and-easy review of the topic.

HOW TO DRAW A MIND MAP

1 First of all, briefly examine the Mind Maps and Mini Mind Maps used in this book. What are the common characteristics? All of them use small pictures or symbols, with words branching out from the illustration.

2 Decide which idea or character in the play you want to illustrate and draw a picture, starting in the middle of the page so that you have plenty of room to branch out. Remember that no one expects a young Rembrandt or Picasso here; artistic ability is not as important as creating an image you (and you alone) will remember. A round smiling (or sad) face might work as well in your memory as a finished portrait. Use marking pens of different colors to make your Mind Map as vivid and memorable as possible.

3 As your thoughts flow freely, add descriptive words and other ideas on the colored branching lines that connect to the central image. Print clearly, using one word per line, if possible.

4 Further refine your thinking by adding smaller branching lines, containing less important facts and ideas, to the main points.

5 Presto! You have a personal outline of your thoughts about the character and plot. It's not a stiff formal outline, but a colorful image that will stick in your mind, it is hoped, throughout classroom discussions and final exams.

HOW TO READ A MIND MAP

1 Begin in the center, the focus of your topic.
2 The words/images attached to the center are like chapter headings; read them next.
3 Always read out from the center, in every direction (even on the left-hand side, where you will have to read from right to left, instead of the usual left to right).

USING MIND MAPS

Mind Maps are a versatile tool; use them for taking notes in class or from books, for solving problems, for brainstorming with friends, and for reviewing and working for tests or exams – their uses are endless! You will find them invaluable for planning essays for coursework and exams. Number your main branches in the order in which you want to use them and off you go – the main headings for your essay are done and all your ideas are logically organized!

Preparing for tests and exams

◆ Review your work systematically. Study hard at the start of your course, not the end, and avoid "exam panic."

◆ Use Mind Maps throughout your course, and build a Master Mind Map for each subject – a giant Mind Map that summarizes everything you know about the subject.

◆ Use memory techniques such as mnemonics (verses or systems for remembering things like dates and events).

◆ Get together with one or two friends to study, compare Mind Maps, and discuss topics.

AND FINALLY...

Have *fun* while you learn – it has been shown that students who make their studies enjoyable understand and remember everything better and get the highest grades. I wish you and your brain every success!

(Tony Buzan)

This guide assumes that you have already read *A Midsummer Night's Dream*, although you could read Background and The Story of *A Midsummer Night's Dream* before that. It is best to use the guide alongside the play. You could read the Who's Who? and Themes sections without referring to the play, but you will get more out of these sections if you do refer to it to check the points made, and especially when thinking about the questions designed to test your recall and help you think about the play.

About the different sections

The Commentary section can be used in a number of ways. One way is to read a scene or part of a scene in the play, and then read the Commentary for that section. Continue until you come to a test section, test yourself – and then take a break. Or, read the Commentary for a scene or part of a scene, then read that section in the play, then go back to the Commentary. Find out what works best for you.

Topics for Discussion or Brainstorming gives topics that could well appear on exams or provide the basis for coursework. It would be particularly useful for you to discuss them with friends, or brainstorm them using Mind Map techniques (see p. vii).

How to Get an "A" in English Literature gives valuable advice on what to look for in a text, and what skills you need to develop in order to achieve your personal best.

The Exam Essay is a useful reminder of how to tackle exam questions, and Model Answer and Essay Plan gives an example of an "A"-grade essay and the Mind Map and plan used to write it.

The questions

Whenever you come across a question with a star ✪ in front of it, think about it for a moment. You could even jot down a few words to focus your mind. There is not usually a "right" answer to these questions; it is important for you to develop your own opinions if you want to get an "A." The Test Yourself sections are designed to take you about 10–20 minutes each, which will be time well spent. Take a short break after each one.

KEY TO ICONS

Themes

A **theme** is an idea explored by an author. Whenever a theme is dealt with in the guide, the appropriate icon is used. This means you can find where a theme is just by flicking through the book. Try it now!

Love

Theater

Authority

Perception

Change

Symbols

In addition to such clear, well-defined themes, Shakespeare also explores bigger ideas that cannot be so clearly defined. Instead, he uses **symbols**: **images** (word pictures), even places, around which there are different associations. For example, Athens in the play is, at its most straightforward level, a city, and the scene for certain parts of the action. As we read the play, however, we find that the idea of Athens suggests much more: notions of order, routine, reality, and other things seem to cluster around it, just as notions of disorder, disruption, and dreams are associated with the idea of the Wood (woods). These symbols are discussed further in the How It Works chapter of this book, and you can trace their progress through the play with the following icons:

Athens

Day

Woods

Night

STYLE AND LANGUAGE

This icon is used in the Commentary wherever there is a special section on the author's choice of words and **imagery**, (the kind of word picture used to make an idea come alive).

SHAKESPEARE'S USE OF VERSE AND PROSE

Shakespeare writes in different ways in *A Midsummer Night's Dream*, according to who is speaking, and the mood the speaker is communicating. The standard verse form, in this as in other Shakespeare plays, is the unrhymed **iambic pentameter** (or blank verse), which has five pairs of syllables to a line, the stress coming always on the second syllable. (See, for example, act 1, scene 1, lines 219–220, where Hermia says *And in the wood where often you and I/Upon faint primrose beds were wont to lie. ...* She is recalling a vision of peaceful privacy, and the absolute regularity of these lines helps convey this impression to her listener.) As often as not, though, Shakespeare will play with this basic rhythm for variety or emphasis. (For instance, line 222 in the same scene starts with a stress on *There*, which gives us a sense of Hermia's resolution. The regularity of the rhythm breaks up more noticeably three lines later (225): *Farewell, sweet playfellow. Pray thou for us....* Here, of course, Hermia is winding up her speech, about to leave, and the rhythm of her speech helps to signal this.)

There are other verse forms too, of course. The rhymed songs of Titania's fairy companions at the start of act 2, scene 2 seem to lull us into calm, where Robin's brutally simple, short-lined rhyming verse later (*Through the forest have I gone,/But Athenian found I none,* act 2, scene 2, lines 72–73) suggests his unsettling quickness. In contrast, the rhyming monotony of the verse in the mechanicals' play, *Pyramus and Thisbe*, underlines its actors' lack of sophistication. Elsewhere, Bottom and his friend speak in **prose** for the most part, their speech thus helping to mark the difference between themselves and their verse-speaking social "superiors."

By using such a range of verse forms, Shakespeare keeps his play alive, and full of rhythmic variety. More than that, though, the rhythms of his verse help reflect the characters of his different speakers, and the changing moods of the play.

When and why

A Midsummer Night's Dream was written in the mid-1590s – 1595 or 1596, we are not sure which. Some experts believe it was specially written to have its first performance not at Shakespeare's regular theater, the Globe, in Southwark, London, but in the gardens of a great country house, as the climax to the celebrations for a big aristocratic wedding. This would certainly have made a lot of sense. It would have meant that, as the newly wed King Theseus and Hippolyta, Lysander and Hermia, and Demetrius and Helena watched Bottom and his friends performing Pyramus and Thisbe, they were being watched in turn by a real-life bride and groom! Robin (also known as Puck), Oberon, and Titania's final blessing (act 5, scene 1, line 388 on) would then have doubled as a blessing on this young couple, their house, and their future family. As we see in the How It Works chapter (p. 20), the social continuity that the institution of marriage represents is one of the central concerns of A Midsummer Night's Dream.

The social order – from top to Bottom

This social continuity is, in turn, part of the wider social order that a grand country house would also have represented. A garden setting, with flowers, grassy banks, and shrubberies, would, of course, have provided the perfect setting for the woodland action of the play. More than this, though, the house and the garden – perhaps bordered by parkland or a forest – would have elegantly embodied the opposition between civilized Athens and the wild "Wood" upon which the play hinges.

THE ARISTOCRACY

Like any family home in Shakespearean England, such a house would have stood for the domestic authority of the father and the husband, and for that of the aristocratic ruling class over the common people.

THE MONARCHY

The monarch stood in the same relation to the country as the father did to his family. Royal authority, like authority in general, was taken to be masculine by definition. The fact that Elizabeth I, England's ruler when *A Midsummer Night's Dream* was first performed, was perhaps England's strongest, most successful monarch ever made no difference. She herself accepted this: "I know I have the body of a weak and feeble woman," she once said, "but I have the heart and stomach of a king."

THE LOWER SOCIAL CLASSES

The house servants and peasantry – perhaps invited to stand respectfully in the background and watch this first performance from a discreet distance – were strictly subordinate, but nevertheless a part of the wider picture. They had to know their place in a rigid class hierarchy, but they did have a place: Without their labor, the whole social structure would have come crashing down. One reason for Shakespeare's inclusion of Bottom and his friends in *A Midsummer Night's Dream* was, of course, the opportunity they afforded for some enjoyable comedy. Another was that their play allowed him to explore the whole question of what theatrical performance is about (see also p. 30). A third reason, though, was that this lower-class contingent completed the picture of social order that was central to the Elizabethan vision. With Bottom and his friends in place, every level of the hierarchy is present in the play. *A Midsummer Night's Dream* may seem like a fantastic fairy tale, but it portrays a whole society, from top to bottom.

The natural and the supernatural

A rural setting for the play's premiere would also have been appropriate given the closeness to ordinary country people of the natural – and the supernatural – worlds.

DO YOU BELIEVE IN FAIRIES?

An enjoyable fantasy today, fairies still had a very real place in the minds of uneducated country people in Shakespeare's time. Their fairies tended to be life-sized and mischievous (even malicious) pranksters – Robin to a T, in other words! The miniaturism of Mustardseed, Mote, Peaseblossom, and Cobweb represents a concession to the tastes of a more sophisticated audience who would not have taken the supernatural too seriously. Although Titania's tiny servitors (male servants) are precisely what we think of when we think of fairies at all, this stereotype would have been new to Shakespeare's audience. Some historians think he invented the modern fairy right here, in *A Midsummer Night's Dream*. So, from Tinkerbell to the Tooth Fairy, it all started here!

1 Theseus tells Hermia she must do as her father says and marry Demetrius

2 Helena tells Demetrius that Hermia intends to elope with Lysander

3 Mechanicals agree to rehearse their play in the woods the next night

4 Oberon and Titania quarrel

5 Oberon sees Demetrius spurn Helena; sends Robin to treat him with magic herbs

6 Oberon treats Titania with herb

4

7 Robin mistakenly treats Lysander

8 Lysander wakes and falls in love with Helena

9 Robin gives Bottom an ass's head. Titania wakes, and falls in love with him

10 Oberon sees how badly Athenians have been treated. Sends Robin to treat Demetrius

11 Hermia and Helena quarrel; Demetrius and Lysander go to fight duel over Helena

12 Oberon brings harmony to lovers and frees Titania from spell. Bottom gets his old head back

13 Theseus says couples should all be married at same ceremony

14 Grand performance of Pyramus and Thisbe; newlyweds go to bed; Oberon, Titania, and Robin bless the marriages

Act 1

Scene 1   Theseus and Hippolyta look forward to their wedding; Egeus accuses Lysander of stealing his daughter, Hermia, who is supposed to be marrying Demetrius. Theseus takes Egeus's side, but Hermia and Lysander resolve, despite this, to run away together. Their friend Helena, who herself loves Demetrius, decides to betray them. If she tells Demetrius what they are planning, she reasons, he will be grateful to her.

Scene 2   A group of Athenian tradesmen plan a performance for the royal wedding celebrations; they agree to meet the following night to rehearse in the woods outside the city.

Act 2

Scene 1   Robin, jester to the Fairy King Oberon, warns a fairy servant of Queen Titania's of his master's rage over the queen's "theft" of a boy-companion. The royal couple meet and quarrel; Oberon plans revenge and sends Robin to find a magic herb that will make the sleeping Titania fall in love with the first thing she sees on waking. Oberon then sees an Athenian youth (Demetrius) being followed by a desperate maiden (Helena), and sends the returning Robin after them, so that the magic can be worked on the unfeeling young man as well.

Scene 2   As Titania sleeps, Oberon squeezes some juice from the herb onto her eye; meanwhile, Lysander and Hermia arrive, lost and exhausted. They decide to lie down and sleep until daylight, lying chastely apart, since they are still unmarried. Finding them like this, Robin assumes that they must be the couple his master had sent him after, and he treats Lysander with the drug. As a result, when Helena now wakes him, Lysander falls head over heels in love with *her*. Helena assumes it's a sick joke, and runs away, but lovesick Lysander takes off after her, leaving Hermia to wake up abandoned and alone.

Act 3

Scene 1 The tradesmen have gathered in the woods to rehearse their play; Robin gives Bottom, the Weaver, an ass's head, and the others flee in alarm. Titania wakes up, sees Bottom, and falls instantly in love.

Scene 2 Robin is telling Oberon what he has done, but when Demetrius comes in with Hermia, who is accusing him of having murdered Lysander, it is apparent that Robin has treated the wrong couple. When Demetrius, left alone by Hermia, lies down to sleep, Robin has a second chance to get things right. This time, Helena arrives; already being pestered by Lysander, she now finds Demetrius also declaring his love. Hermia returns, accusing her of stealing Lysander's love, and Helena concludes that her former friends must have joined together to taunt her. As the women quarrel, the men go off to fight a duel over Helena. Oberon tells Robin to lead the lovers off through the woods until each has been matched with the right partner.

Act 4

Scene 1 Taking pity on his queen, Oberon releases Titania from her spell and they are reconciled. He gives Bottom his own head back, and leaves him sleeping. Theseus, Hippolyta, and Egeus arrive in the woods for a dawn hunt. They find and wake the sleeping young people, now perfectly matched in love: Demetrius with Helena, and Lysander with Hermia. Egeus is angry, but Demetrius says that he is happy with the way things have turned out. Theseus rules that the lovers should all be married in the same ceremony as he and Hippolyta. Bottom wakes up, astonished, and rushes off to tell the story of his amazing dream.

Scene 2 The other workmen are agitated at the transformation of Bottom and the resulting collapse of their venture into the field of drama. Bottom arrives, back in his old form. He has wonders to reveal, he says, but it will have to wait, since their play has been chosen for a performance at the royal wedding celebrations.

7

Act 5

Scene 1 It is the evening of the next day, and the newlyweds, Theseus and Hippolyta, are discussing what they have been hearing about the events of the night before. Theseus is skeptical: he thinks it is all just the imagination of young love run wild. Egeus arrives with news of the entertainment being offered. Theseus is in favor of the workmen's *Pyramus and Thisbe*, though Egeus tries to persuade him not to be. The play goes on, and is every bit as bad as Egeus has predicted, but it is still good-naturedly received. Theseus draws the celebrations to a close, and the mortals go off to bed, leaving the stage to Oberon, Titania, and Robin, who bless the house and promise their protection to the newly married couples.

HOW MUCH CAN YOU REMEMBER?

Try to fill in the words missing from this alternative summary without looking back at the original. Feel free to use your own words if they have the same meaning.

Act 1

Scene 1 Theseus and Hippolyta look forward to their _____ ; Egeus accuses Lysander of stealing his daughter, _____ , who is, he says, supposed to be marrying _____ . Theseus takes Egeus's side, but the young lovers decide to run away together. Their friend _____ resolves to betray them to _____ .

Scene 2 Some tradesmen plan to rehearse a play. They will meet next night in the _____ outside the city.

Act 2

Scene 1 Robin, jester to the Fairy King _____ , says his master is furious with Queen _____ . The royal couple meet and quarrel; the king plans revenge and sends Robin to find a _____ that will make the sleeping queen fall in love with the first thing she sees when she wakes up. The king sees an

Athenian youth (_____) being followed by a desperate maiden (_____) and decides to help.

Scene 2 As Titania sleeps, Oberon squeezes juice from the herb onto her eye; meanwhile, _____ and Hermia, lost and exhausted, lie down and sleep. Finding them, _____ assumes they must be the couple his master wanted him to treat with the herb, so he anoints _____ 's eyes with the drug. When _____ arrives and wakes him, Demetrius, having finally managed to shake off her pursuit, _____ falls head over heels in love with *her*. They go off, and _____ is left all alone.

Act 3

Scene 1 The tradesmen are in the woods rehearsing their play; Robin gives _____ an ass's head, and the others flee in alarm. Titania wakes up, sees him, and falls instantly in love.

Scene 2 Robin tells _____ what he has done, but when Demetrius comes in with _____ , who is accusing him of having murdered Lysander, it becomes clear that Robin has treated the wrong couple. Left alone by Hermia, Demetrius lies down to sleep, so Robin has a second chance to get things right. This time, _____ arrives; already being pestered by Lysander, she now finds Demetrius also declaring his love. Hermia returns, saying her old friend has stolen Lysander's love, and _____ concludes that her former friends must have joined together to taunt her. As the women quarrel, the men go off to fight a duel over Helena. Oberon tells _____ to lead the lovers off through the woods until each has been matched with the right partner.

Act 4

Scene 1 Taking pity, _____ releases Titania from her spell. He gives _____ his own head back, leaving him sleeping. _____ , Hippolyta, and Egeus arrive in the woods for a dawn hunt. They find the young people, now perfectly matched in love: Demetrius with _____ , and Lysander with _____ . Egeus is angry, but _____ rules that the lovers should share a wedding with himself and Hippolyta. Bottom wakes up, astonished.

Scene 2   The other workmen are agitated at the transformation of Bottom, but he promptly arrives, back in his old form. He has wonders to reveal, he says, but it will have to wait, since their play, _____ *and* _____ , has been chosen for a performance at the royal wedding celebrations.

Act 5

Theseus and _____ are talking about the strange stories they have heard about the events of the night before. Egeus tells him of the entertainment being offered and Theseus is in favor of *Pyramus and* _____. The play is performed, then Theseus draws the celebrations to a close and the mortals go to bed, leaving the stage to Oberon, Titania, and _____ , who bless the newly married couples.

now that you've read the plot, take a break before finding out who's who

WHO'S WHO?

The Mini Mind Map above summarizes the character groups in *A Midsummer Night's Dream*. Test yourself by looking at the full Mind Map on p. 19, and then copying the Mini Mind Map and trying to add to it from memory.

HOW TO REMEMBER WHO'S WHO

It can be hard at first to tell which character is which in *A Midsummer Night's Dream*, so think of nicknames that will help you do the job. The young lovers seem more or less interchangeable at first, though the distinctions are crucial and with time will become clear. There is all the difference in the world between Lyrical Lysander and Dour Demetrius. Of the women, meanwhile, Hapless Helena has a *Hell*ish time for much of the play, whereas everyone seems to want Heavenly Hermia. Aged Egeus is Hermia's possessive father. It is harder to think of nicknames for Theseus and Hippolyta, but then it's harder to forget who they are. And while it isn't easy to remember which workman is which, you don't really have to, since they form a company of equals, none of whom takes on any strongly individual identity – except, of course, for Bottom, and if you can't remember his name then you really *do* have problems!

Noble mortals

Theseus

The Duke of Athens, Theseus is a brisk, businesslike man, used to power and authority. He embodies the world of the daytime city – a world of law, order, and matter-of-fact clarity. It is significant that he will not enter the nighttime woods that are the setting for the play's main enchanted action. Instead, the arrival of his hunting party (act 4, scene 1) will signal the restoration of daytime order. Theseus's problem is that he lacks imagination. It is ironic, then, that this down-to-earth detachment should enable him to give the play's most thoughtful (and, in its firmly antipoetic way, poetic) summary of what the imagination involves and is capable of (act 5, scene 1, lines 2–28).

It is ironic, too, that *Pyramus and Thisbe*, the play within the play of *A Midsummer Night's Dream*, is conceived, written, and finally staged in Theseus's honor. Like any government, Theseus has an arts policy; he senses that events and spectacles are essential to a society's sense of itself. He recognizes the importance of entertainment, even though he himself may not be able to enter imaginatively into the darker, more thrilling, and more disturbing dimensions that art opens up.

Hippolyta

Theseus's bride-to-be, Hippolyta, is not the easiest of characters to pin down, not that you have to, of course – her ambiguity only makes her more interesting. She doesn't seem obviously upset in act 1, scene 1 at the prospect of marrying Theseus (though there could be a hint in lines 7–8 that the time that is passing so slowly for Theseus cannot pass slowly enough for her). It is worth bearing in mind, though, that the marriage with Theseus was not her idea. In Greek mythology, Hippolyta was the Queen of the Amazons, a race of fiercely independent women warriors who rejected men. They were finally defeated in battle by the forces of Theseus, so Hippolyta comes to the duke as a trophy of war. Her marriage to him symbolizes her own surrender, and her man-hating nation's subjection, to the authority of Theseus and Athens. (Theseus touches on this in act 1, scene 1, lines 120–121.)

What this says about the play's view of love and marriage is a matter of interpretation. On the one hand you could argue that Shakespeare presents the Amazons' self-sufficiency, and thus female chastity in general, as a barren, fruitless, self-centered state that must be brought to an end, by force if necessary. Theseus certainly speaks of it in these terms to Hermia, act 1, scene 1, lines 72, 74. How is humankind to continue, after all, if women refuse to have children? On the other hand, you could see the play as highlighting the oppression of women by men, presenting marriage as a straightforward subjection of women, backed up by law and the threat of force.

Egeus

If Theseus represents the authority of the state and the law, Hermia's father, Egeus, stands for paternal authority within the family. But just as the limitations of Theseus's worldly order will be highlighted by the revelation of a parallel world of dream and magic, in which his earthbound authority is not recognized, Egeus, too, will have to accept that his power over his daughter has its limits. His is a possessive, even savage love; in act 1, scene 1, line 45, he makes it clear he is prepared to contemplate the idea of his daughter's death rather than accept her disobedience. ✪ Do you think she owes him any obedience at all?

This paternal authority is upheld by Theseus as the play begins, but then, as Egeus's own language makes clear (act 1, scene 1, lines 98–100), wider principles of property and law are at stake: What will happen to the fabric of society if its daughters are going to start disposing of themselves in marriage, making nonsense of any contractual agreements their fathers may have made? By act 4, scene 1, though, Demetrius is waiving his claim to Hermia, these principles are no longer threatened, and the duke supports Hermia's marriage with Lysander. *Egeus, I will overbear your will*, he says (act 4, scene 1, line 186). Sometimes, what a character does not say can be as crucial as what he or she does, and

Egeus's silence on this decision is deafening. Like it or not, though, he must give way to a public authority higher than his own private authority.

Hermia

In the romantic comedy that makes up the heart of *A Midsummer Night's Dream*, Hermia seems to have things pretty much her own way. She is loved by the man she herself loves, Lysander, and, indeed, by another man she doesn't – Helena's love, Demetrius. It can be hard to remember as the play goes on that when we first meet Hermia she is under the threat of death or confinement in a convent. For Hermia, though, the play can be seen as a progression from the role of young girl under her father's authority to that of grown woman, able to choose her own husband. Cynics will say that this represents a move from one form of subjection to another, especially if Oberon's crushing of Titania's will (see Titania, on p. 16) is taken as the play's model for marriage. The truth is, of course, that Shakespeare is never as simple as that. You can see these things either way, and in any case, both Hermia and Titania are living, breathing characters; they cannot be reduced to mere symbols of any single view of the world.

Lysander

As a highborn young man, Hermia's love, Lysander, has much invested in his self-image as a gentleman and as a courtly lover. He has mastered the language of romantic love almost too well, only forgetting that the true knight shows his love, finally, not by his words but by the deeds he performs in the service and protection of his maiden.

This idea of himself will be undercut in act 3, scene 1 when, under the influence of Robin's magic, Lysander finds himself behaving in a most ungentlemanly way to the supposed eternal object of his love, Hermia. The excessively flowery language of Lysander's love then is placed under particular scrutiny. It loses much of its credibility once it becomes clear that it can be turned out so easily, and that it consists of praises so preposterously superlative that it leaves the real woman behind and addresses only an abstract ideal.

While Hermia and Helena are two different individuals, as far as the language of love is concerned they seem interchangeable, and while the terms it uses for them are flattering (see act 3, scene 2, both Lysander's and Demetrius's speeches), they do not convey much about the reality of either woman.

Helena

Of all the young lovers, Helena is the one who seems most to resist the spell of the woods. She is the only one who does not at any point in the night fall asleep, which in the other characters can be seen as marking the moment of victory for the woods' magic powers. Helena has good reason for her more realistic attitude, though, having been so thwarted to begin with. It is as though the earlier loss of Demetrius's love leaves Helena literally "disenchanted" and therefore unenchantable; she starts off in despair, while Demetrius, Lysander, and Hermia all enter the woods in hopes of one thing or another. It is ironic that, as the night approaches its end, she will be the one whose midsummer night's dream has come true – having the love of both young men she finds herself in Hermia's former situation, which she found so enviable in act 1, scene 1, lines 196–197; however, it doesn't give her what she wanted.

Demetrius

Although the least clearly distinct of the young Athenians, Demetrius does develop during the course of the play. In act 1, scene 1 he claims to love Hermia but the way he demands her as if in completion of a deal does not suggest strong feelings on his part and shows complete indifference to any feelings she might have herself. This egotism is imprisoning. So long as he is in thrall to it, the love of another person is no more than an irritating nuisance, hence the bitter near-violence of his treatment of Helena in act 2, scene 1. Robin's magic frees him from his own selfishness, allowing him to appreciate the value of the love Helena offers him, and through that to discover depths in his own character. The Demetrius who speaks so lovingly of Helena and so wonderingly of his night's experiences at the end of act 4, scene 2 is not the cold, legalistic speaker of act 1, scene 1.

Fairies

Oberon

Theseus's counterpart in Fairyland, King Oberon, is also the presiding genius behind the enchanted action in the nighttime woods. He attempts to work the other characters like the cast in his own little play. His spells are responsible for the action we see, making a spectacle of the queen with Bottom and organizing the romantic lives of Hermia, Lysander, Helena, and Demetrius. In that sense, he can be seen as a playwright within the play, a stand-in for Shakespeare. The difference, of course, is that Oberon has nowhere near the skill as a dramatist. Though he produces an amusing (if unsophisticated) comedy in the case of Titania and Bottom, the joyous romantic comedy he envisages for the young Athenians ends up in a hopeless tangle. Like the author of *Pyramus and Thisbe*, Oberon teaches us how *not* to write a play, and thus helps us to better appreciate the all-but-magical accomplishment behind a play that really works.

The ultimate proof of Oberon's inadequacy as a playwright is his inability to stomach his own creation. As we shall see in act 4, scene 1, line 50, when he calls the innocent Bottom "hateful," Oberon cannot actually endure the sight of his queen with the monster his assistant has created. By line 76, however, Oberon has clearly moved beyond such negative notions as that of hatefulness. In a much more positive mood, he calls on Titania to *Be as thou wast wont to be,/ See as thou wast wont to see* (lines 72–73). These lines imply an acceptance of Titania exactly "as she was," faults and all. Oberon, who thought that he was the one dispensing the magic during this night of enchantment, has himself been changed by the experience, although the change, ironically, is to an acceptance of how things were to begin with!

Titania

Although so many of the play's main characters are on the brink of marriage, and their wedding celebrations will indeed constitute its conclusion, Titania and Oberon's is actually the play's only real, up-and-running marriage. Not that they are very good role models; the Fairyland action opens (act 2, scene 1) with the royal couple so much at odds that they have separated, and while it will conclude with their loving reconciliation (act 4, scene 1), the means by which that reconciliation has been brought about are questionable, to say the least.

A willful, wayward wife, Titania disobeys her husband and is punished with humiliation. We should not let the humor of her dalliance with Bottom blind us to the cruelty of her punishment. Magnanimous as Oberon may feel by act 4, scene 1, he was not prepared to take this view until he had won Titania's surrender (line 57). Marital harmony, according to this view of Oberon's behavior, depends strictly on the man remaining in charge; thus the royal marriage in Fairyland raises the same issues as its Athenian equivalent (see Hippolyta, p. 12). Is marriage about equal sharing or dominance and submission? ✪ What do you think?

Robin (Puck)

General factotum to the Fairy King, Robin embodies the spirit of mischief in Fairyland. Shakespeare took this character directly from the folk tradition, in which from time immemorial he had worked his wicked tricks. Puck was also often called Robin Goodfellow, in a spirit partly of fearful flattery (if they were nice enough about him, people hoped, he might spare them his attentions), and partly, too, of **irony**, given that, far from being a "good fellow," he was a thoroughly bad character. (In much the same spirit, of course, modern American gangsters have been referred to as "goodfellas.") Robin of *A Midsummer Night's Dream* is true to tradition. Along with an undisputed sense of humor, he also has a distinctly cruel streak, as the practical joke he describes in act 2, scene 1, lines 49–60, for instance, illustrates. The misery caused to the mortal lovers when his plan unravels upsets Oberon; as far as Robin is concerned, however, it just makes things that much more fun (act 3, scene 2, lines 373–374). In addition to all his other faults, Robin is a snob, describing the workmen in act 3, scene 2, lines 9–10 as *A crew of patches, rude mechanicals*. The fact that they *work for bread upon Athenian stalls* damns them in his eyes, though we might respect them for it.

The venom with which Robin talks here is initially surprising; what did these inoffensive souls ever do to him? The answer perhaps lies in his own peculiar status. His supernatural powers may be phenomenal, but he remains a servant. Theseus, Hippolyta, and the young lovers are all of high, if human, birth, and all have been taken under the protection of the Fairy King. These *rude mechanicals*, as Robin calls them (act 3, scene 2, line 9) are perhaps the only characters in the play to whom he can feel securely superior.

Bottom and the mechanicals

The *mechanicals* can be seen as constituting a single collective character; it is not just that Shakespeare has not made the effort to portray them as individuals (though it is for the most part true; he hasn't). Rather, as can be seen in the informal, democratic way in which they rehearse their play (act 1, scene 2; act 3, scene 1), these working-class men seem naturally to operate as a team, all for one and one for all. Bottom is the most (if not the only) developed individual character among them, and it is clear from act 4, scene 2 that his friends look up to him as someone special.

To us, of course, just about everything about Bottom can seem absurd, from his name to his lack of education, to his swaggering sense of his own importance. Yet the man who wants "Bottom's Dream" to be made into a ballad with himself as the hero (act 4, scene 1, lines 224–227) has worthwhile qualities too. There is something comic about his concern that his fairy servitor should not be overwhelmed by the contents of the bumblebee's honeysac he has sent him to get (act 4, scene 1, lines 15–17), but there is also something touching. Lowborn, vulgar, and grossly physical as he admittedly is, Bottom displays a native nobility that his social "betters" do not always match.

now that you know your Helena from your Hermia, take a break before seeing how it all fits together

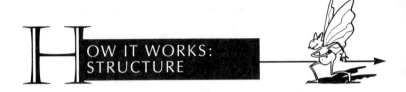

How it Works: Structure

Although the action in *A Midsummer Night's Dream* keeps moving excitingly along through all five acts, it is nevertheless noticeable that the serious drama reaches its conclusion long before the actual play does. As early as act 3, scene 2, lines 397–398, Oberon makes clear his intentions of having everything turn out all right. The action of act 4 is accordingly devoted to the release of Titania from her humiliating delusion and the untangling of the knots the young lovers have been left in, first, by Demetrius's perverse spurning of Helena and turning to Hermia, and second, by Robin's misguided intervention. Act 5 largely consists of a happy reunion of the cast, finding both young lovers and mechanicals back in Athens, where the groups will have their only meeting as actors and audience at the court of Theseus, under the benevolent protection of the Fairy King and Queen.

A CIRCULAR ARGUMENT

So, if the drama is over only halfway through the play, why does the whole thing not simply fall flat? Usually, we know, a dramatist tries to build tension as the play goes on, until it reaches its end in a smashing climax. *A Midsummer Night's Dream*, though, does not present things in such a "linear" fashion. While obviously, as in any play, the action has to be staged as a series of events taking place one after another in time, the dynamic energy of this play pushes in quite a different direction. The emotional heart of *A Midsummer Night's Dream* is its structural heart, its center. The concentric circles of Figure 1 (p. 21) tell us much more about the progress of the play than any linear plot summary could.

DAY 1 ATHENS V. NIGHT/WOODS

In the diagram the outer circle represents the daytime world of Athens, a state of disciplined order and down-to-earth reality. The inner circle represents the nighttime woods, Oberon's

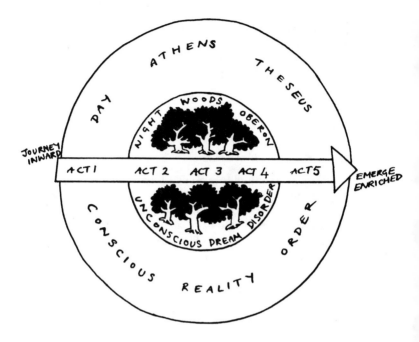

Figure 1

kingdom, a dark world of disorder and away-with-the-fairies fantasy. Psychologically, the move from Athens to the woods can be seen as an inward journey from the conscious to the unconscious level. Though the irredeemably rational, orderly Theseus has to remain in the outer zone throughout, with Hippolyta and Egeus, the other two main groups among the mortals – the ardent young lovers and the innocent, unsophisticated mechanicals – both go into the woods and have their very different experiences in it. Emerging during act 4, they find themselves right back where they started, in Athens, unsure as they return groggily to consciousness whether their journey has taken place at all. It has though, we know. For one thing, the tangled affections of Hermia, Lysander, Helena, and Demetrius have sorted themselves out as if by magic. For another, the Athens of act 5 is a subtly different place from the Athens of act 1; there is an energy, a crackling charge in act 5, scene 1 that wasn't there before. At its most basic you can see it as the sexual tension of three couples on the brink of their first marital bedtime. More than this, though, it is a mark of how the conscious, everyday level of life is enhanced by any touch of enchantment, whether the magic comes in the form of actual spells or in their equivalents: romantic love, dream, or, as in *A Midsummer Night's Dream*, art.

OPPOSITES AT WORK

Figure 2, on p. 23, shows some of the opposites at work in *A Midsummer Night's Dream* between these two symbolic orders of existence: Theseus's world of daytime Athens and Oberon's nighttime woods. These opposites are not, of course, presented in such an obvious way in Shakespeare's text (you can trace them through the action by the Athens, Woods, Day, and Night icons in the Commentary section), but it is nevertheless revealing to view them as they are laid out here, for they are important underlying principles in *A Midsummer Night's Dream*. It is another aspect of the play's nonlinearity that it does not move simply from one side of the table to the other – from the conscious to the unconscious, say, or vice versa – but holds both simultaneously in suspension, finding each indispensable to life.

SHAKESPEAREAN CYCLES

You cannot, Shakespeare's play suggests, have clear, matter-of-fact consciousness without a dark, dreamy unconscious, any more than you can have day without night. The dominant movement in *A Midsummer Night's Dream* is thus not one of progression from start to finish, but of cycles – the never-ending cycles of the sun that give us days and nights; the phases of the moon that mark our months; the seasons of the year; and, of course, the wider cycles by which men and women are born, grow up, and die, having brought into the world, meanwhile, the new babies of generations to come. See Figure 3 – The Bard on a Bike, p. 24.

CONSCIOUS	UNCONSCIOUS
LIGHT	DARK
REALITY	DREAM
CLARITY	MYSTERY
OPENNESS	CONCEALMENT
ORDER	DISORDER
LAW	LICENSE
DUTY	DESIRE
ROUTINE	DISRUPTION
MUNDANE	MAGIC
LIFE	ART
PROSE	POETRY

Figure 2

LIFE GOES ON

Such cycles are central, not merely to *A Midsummer Night's Dream*, but to Shakespearean comedy in general. Comedy isn't all laughs, nor does it necessarily even involve more light than dark. The point is, rather, that it reassures us that life goes on. Death is not absent from the world of comedy; it is just that in this world it leads to rebirth, as night does to day. These

23

Figure 3   Bard on a bike

continuities are collective. Each of us individually may grow old and die, but society survives. The life of the individual is finite, will end in that individual's death, and is therefore tragic. (Think of Shakespeare's great tragedies, for the most part each named for a single person – *Hamlet*, *Othello*, *King Lear*, or *Macbeth*.) Comedy, by contrast, celebrates the endurance of the community. That is why, instead of building suspense or tension in a linear narrative, *A Midsummer Night's Dream* seems to go around in circles, and ends, since it must, as a stage play, end somewhere, not with some dramatic confrontation but with an act of collective celebration that brings together all levels of society, from the lowest to the highest – even the immortals.

now relax and give yourself a chance to unwind a little – or you'll end up going around in circles yourself!

A theme is an idea developed or explored throughout a work. The main themes of *A Midsummer Night's Dream* are shown in the Mini Mind Map above. "Imagery" refers to the kind of word picture used to bring the themes to life. Test yourself on the themes by copying the Mini Mind Map above, adding to it yourself, and then comparing your results with the full Mind Map on p. 34.

Love

Love, they say, makes the world go around, and since, as we saw in the previous section, *A Midsummer Night's Dream* is a play built around cycles, that is appropriate enough. Without the love that leads men and women to come together and produce and rear families, the world – as far as the human race is concerned, at any rate – would grind to a halt. The love that underpins the institution of marriage comprises both desire and devotion. Without the first, men and women would never produce children; the second is essential if those children are then to be successfully raised. Love within the family comes in different forms, of course. Egeus's paternal love for his daughter, Hermia, is tied up with ideas of authority, duty, and law; in act 1, scene 1, lines 152–157 Hermia will turn the tables, presenting the love she feels for Lysander as a law unto itself.

Both are right in a sense. You must consider for yourself how far Hermia is right to follow the law of love. Arguably, Egeus has a right to require his daughter's obedience until she is old enough to make up her own mind, and she has a right to leave her immediate family for the man she loves when she is sure that it is time to do so.

LOVE AND DUTY

For society's sake, love does have to submit to discipline; comic as it is, Titania's infatuation with the modified Bottom offers a more serious warning, too, of what monstrosities might come about if certain boundaries are not observed. At the same time, though, love has to have the courage to break a few rules. If every girl in Hermia's position were to submit meekly to her father's natural possessiveness, the human race would die out. So it has always been: love winning out, but never without a struggle.

LOVE AND CONFLICT

But then, conflict and love go hand in hand. If good marriages, like good friendships, involve mutual respect and cooperation, they can also involve possessiveness and jealousy, negative feelings that deform closeness and affection. The best of friendships, meanwhile, can be undermined by love. See how the good-hearted Helena starts plotting against her friend, Hermia, at the end of act 1, scene 1, and how Helena, in turn, complains of Hermia's betrayal during their quarrel in the woods (act 3, scene 2, lines 197–365).

LOVE AND POETRY

Love is traditionally associated with poetry, too, with flowery compliments and extravagant vows. As Lysander's example so often shows, however, these can take flight to such an extent that the language of love is emptied of meaning. In act 3, scene 2, we see how Hermia and Helena become, to all intents and purposes, interchangeable in the language of Demetrius and Lysander: The young men's compliments are so ridiculously poetic that they will fit either woman equally well – or badly. Likewise, we see how the terms in which Lysander expresses his "false" love – the feelings Robin's magic have given him for Helena – are indistinguishable from those in which he expresses his "true" love for Hermia. With all this rhetoric, the beloved herself is all but forgotten, as Lysander's beloved Hermia finds herself forgotten in act 2, scene 2, lines 152–163.

ROMANTIC CHALLENGES

While the challenge Lysander faces in the play is that of bringing his love back down to earth from the realm of empty eloquence to that of living, breathing life, the task for Demetrius, as we saw in his Who's Who? entry on p. 15, is to acquire a bit of romance. He has to learn to stop seeing love as a glorified business deal. His wondering thought, in act 4, scene 1, lines 194–195, that the things he now sees around him seem *Like far-off mountains turnèd into clouds*, shows us that, along with a true appreciation of Helena and her love, he has gained a new way of looking at his world. True love changes us, as it does both Lysander and Demetrius, helping us reach beyond our normal limitations to our "better selves."

Authority

Authority takes a number of different forms in *A Midsummer Night's Dream*. The play calls into question the authority of the king (Theseus) over his subjects, of the state (Athens) over its citizens, of the father (Egeus) over his child (Hermia), of the husband (Oberon) over his wife (Titania). The elopement of Hermia and Lysander represents a defiance of the first three of these (King, State, and Father). Titania's refusal to return the Indian boy is a rejection of the fourth. The crazy goings-on in the nighttime woods can be seen as upsetting any idea of order or authority altogether. ✪ How far is this really the case? The queen is, of course, humiliatingly punished for her waywardness, but Hermia, surely, is rewarded for hers? So it may seem at first glance.

WHO WEARS THE PANTS?

More carefully considered, though, things are not so simple. While the play may appear to approve of Hermia's romantic rebellion, she will end up subjecting herself to the authority of another man, her husband, Lysander, in marriage. It is true that the men in *A Midsummer Night's Dream* do not always wear the pants; the romantic tradition of poetic love does confer upon the lady an authority of her own, although on a strictly temporary basis. But the Demetrius and Lysander who so exaggeratedly abase themselves to Helena in act 3, scene 2 will probably be just as bad as Oberon once they are married.

BACK TO REALITY

Reveling as it does in the suspension of everyday order, in magical transformations, and escape into dreams, *A Midsummer Night's Dream* nevertheless has its thematic feet firmly on the ground. The disorder of the nighttime woods is liberating, but the lovers must return to the real world to live their lives, just as we have to return from the exhilarating heights of artistic fantasy to the more mundane concerns of everyday life. The trick is to enhance the life we have, not to change it altogether.

As we saw in How It Works on p. 20, *A Midsummer Night's Dream* sees order and disorder as two sides of the same coin. Rules are made to be broken, but only so that the wider principle of order should be maintained. Though some scholars have looked to Shakespeare for radical political messages, they have, for the most part, been disappointed. *A Midsummer Night's Dream*, too, is more conservative than it may immediately seem. Feminists may be inclined to applaud the Amazonian independence of Hippolyta, Hermia's daughterly disobedience, and Titania's feisty insubordination; however, they will be less happy at the thought that Hippolyta is effectively a trophy of war, that Hermia ends up meekly marrying, and that Titania is crushed once more into wifely submission.

In the same way, those who have felt that the mechanicals represent some sort of revolutionary spirit are also, surely, misguided. There is, undoubtedly, a real sense of energy about Bottom and his friends, and they do, among themselves, show a splendidly democratic spirit of mutual loyalty and cooperation. There is never, however, the slightest hint that they hold their social "superiors" in anything other than the highest, most unquestioning regard.

Change

The idea of change is central to *A Midsummer Night's Dream*. The characters are, as we have seen, forced by their experiences to change their views of themselves and each other. Magic changes reality in the woods, throwing the ordinary rules of nature into disorder, allowing Robin (act 2, scene 1, lines 181–182) to *put a girdle round about the earth/ in forty minutes*, giving a man an ass's head and making nonsense of the normal scale of things (think of Bottom and his fairy servitors in act 3, scene 1 and act 4, scene 1, for instance). The poet works magical change when, like Shakespeare in *A Midsummer Night's Dream*, he weaves a world out of words and, as Theseus puts it (act 5, scene 1, lines 17–18), *gives to airy nothing/ A local habitation and a name*.

IMAGES AND SPELLS

As we see in our discussion of act 2, scene 1 in the Commentary on p. 43, the images that change flowers into soldiers or dewdrops into pearls can themselves be seen as spells of a sort, but then, so too can the whole theatrical experience. What is it if not magic that changes a modern actor into an Athenian nobleman, a "rude mechanical," or an Amazon queen? If we are prepared to cooperate ourselves, to play our own part as the audience by using our imagination, the magic they work may even change our lives a little.

Theater

A Midsummer Night's Dream is a work of theater; that is obvious enough, but it is also a work *about* theater. We saw in the preceding section how the play can be seen to highlight the wizardry of writing, the magical powers of performance. In that sense, the play can be seen to celebrate the wonder of art and the theater. It should also be noticed, however, that Shakespeare's play actually contains one play in performance – the mechanicals' production of *Pyramus and Thisbe*. And as we have seen in looking at Oberon (p. 16), the Fairy King's attempts to manipulate the action in the woods can be seen as

a second. Each of these different plays-within-the-play highlights by its clumsiness the all but magical accomplishment of a real playwright like Shakespeare, and the skills involved in bringing a classic drama to the stage: lighting, music, costume, and scenery as well as direction and acting.

THEATER AND SOCIETY

Preposterous as it is, *Pyramus and Thisbe* does demonstrate some of the benefits of the theater: its social value as an activity that brings a community together, whether as audience or as actors, and the opportunities it offers for even those of relatively little education, like Bottom and his friends, to extend horizons otherwise bounded by work. Even the resolutely unimaginative Theseus is aware of this aspect of the theater's importance.

More than a stage play, *A Midsummer Night's Dream* is a glorious tribute to the theater as a whole – to the whole strange business of writing, rehearsal, interpretation, direction, to the magic, living communication between actors and audience. This is why the mechanicals' farcical tragedy should not be dismissed as a trivial "comic subplot," thrown in just to lighten the mood. On the contrary, it is the central performance of a play about plays.

Perception

Reality is perceived in *A Midsummer Night's Dream*, as in life, by the five senses. Any dramatic performance must, of course, appeal to the senses of sight and hearing, but Shakespeare's language in this play thrills the mind's eye too, with images of cowslip soldiers and dewdrop pearls (act 2, scene 1, lines 10, 14–15), and fans made of butterfly wings (act 3, scene 1, lines 178–179), to mention only a few of the poetry's visual miracles. Music is crucial to this play, but our ears are delighted by Shakespeare's verse as well, not just its rhythms but at times, as in Oberon's *I know a bank* speech (act 2, scene 1, lines 256–275), in the very sound of the words. With all its fragrant flowers, that speech appeals to our sense of smell too, as well as to the sense of touch (the warmth and luxurious softness of Titania's couch; the snake's sudden cold).

In act 3, scene 1, lines 172–174, the Fairy Queen orders her servants to bring Bottom a selection of mouthwatering delicacies, appealing to our sense of taste.

REALITY V. ILLUSION

We do not only perceive physically, however. As we saw earlier, Theseus is the play's leading realist. An intelligent but determinedly unimaginative observer, he perceives his prosaic world with complete clarity. Where Theseus uses his head, the other main characters lose theirs. Thinking "with the heart," they leap over the boundaries of "factual" reality into a very different realm of experience. A realm not of objective "truth," but illusion, it is for all that a world of wonder; though it may not be "real" itself, it has the capacity to transform reality.

Love takes the young lovers into an ecstatic world beyond humdrum reality. It enables Demetrius and Lysander, in particular, to transcend their usual limitations and attain their "better selves." Magic and dream are external forces in the nighttime woods, but their effect on the young people is much the same. As for us, as readers or audience, we are not ourselves involved in the characters' story. Yet art, in the form of Shakespeare's play, allows us an experience every bit as magical, every bit as transcendent.

MUSIC AND POETRY

The song and dance in which *A Midsummer Night's Dream* abounds makes it an audiovisual feast, bombarding its audience's senses as well as addressing its mind. It is always important for poetry to appeal to the senses as well as the intellect, but it is especially important in a play that concerns the need to transcend everyday reality, to cross the frontiers of normal thought into the world of dreams and magic.

We are used to language explaining all mystery, all strangeness away, reducing everything to cold common sense. The task the creative writer faces is to help language conquer this side of its own nature, helping us not merely to understand our world but to appreciate its wonder. One of the great gifts of the theater is that it is not bound by its binding as a book is. The written script is only the beginning; in the performance; the play offers not just words and their meanings but actors, voices, sounds, scenery, spectacle.

HEAD V. HEART

So, though it may seem a strange thing to say of a classic work of literature, words in *A Midsummer Night's Dream* are almost a necessary evil. We have to use words, but we will attempt to use them in a way that speaks not to the "head" but to the "heart." Shakespeare reaches beyond the immediate meaning of his words to exploit the music inherent in language – the rhythms of prose and poetry (in a variety of different line lengths and rhyme schemes), the sounds of the words themselves – as well as music itself, sometimes just instrumental, sometimes integrated with his poetry in the form of songs. He seduces the mind with the smells of woodland herbs and flowers, appeals to the sense of touch with his talk of soft beds, gentle breezes, and, on the other hand, cold serpents. Sound, rhythm, and spectacle, all contribute to the effects of the fairies' dances.

All in all, *A Midsummer Night's Dream* is an astonishingly vivid and varied multimedia experience. Not just a great work of art, it is a celebration of art itself.

now put down your Shakespeare and get some exercise, or put on some music – or bombard your senses with a snack.

COMMENTARY

The Commentary looks at each scene in turn, beginning with a brief preview that will prepare you for the scene and help in last minute review. The Commentary comments on whatever is important in the section, focusing on the areas shown in the Mini Mind Map above.

ICONS

Wherever there is a focus on a particular theme, the icon for that theme appears in the margin (see p. xi for key). Look, too, for the Style and Language sections. Being able to comment on style and language will help you to get an "A" on your exam.
You will learn more from the Commentary if you use it alongside the play itself. Read a scene from the play, then the corresponding Commentary section, or the other way around.

QUESTIONS

Remember that when a question appears in the Commentary with a star ✪ in front of it, you should stop and think about it for a moment. And do **remember to take a break** after completing each exercise.

Act 1 scene 1

◆ Theseus and Hippolyta look forward to their wedding.
◆ Egeus accuses Lysander of stealing his daughter, Hermia, who has been promised to Demetrius.
◆ Theseus takes Egeus's side, but Hermia and Lysander resolve to run away together.
◆ Helena, who herself loves Demetrius, decides to betray Hermia and Lysander in order to win Demetrius's gratitude.

☼ Though the play is supposed to be about a midsummer *night's* dream, this opening scene takes place by day. That is reassuring in a way; there can be something frightening about the night and its dark shadows, and it is nice to be able to see everything clearly and know just what is what. At the same time, though, there is less scope for illusion in the "cold light of day," and illusions can be sustaining. By night, in our dreams, we can be anything, anyone, we want. Frightening as it may be, in some ways the night can seem preferable.

The play begins with thoughts of love, Theseus looking forward to his marriage with Hippolyta. His eager anticipation comes through in verse (lines 3–4): *But O, methinks, how slow/This old moon wanes.* Read the lines aloud. Three consecutive stresses on *old moon wanes* slow line 4 down (line 3 skips along by comparison), conveying Theseus's impatience.

FATHER KNOWS BEST?

Egeus appears, spouting his rights under the law, authority, and duty. Suddenly, the mood of the scene becomes more serious. Theseus is not a lover anymore but the duke, the man in charge of laying down the law. If he has private desires, he also has public duties. So does Hermia, he says. She must decide between marriage with the man her father chooses, lifelong virginity in a convent, or death. ✪ What do you think she should do?

Egeus's view is clear. He wants Hermia to marry Demetrius. He tells Lysander (lines 99–100): *And she is mine, and all my right of her/I do estate unto Demetrius.* He talks about his daughter in legal language, as if she were a piece of land or property.

Left behind together, Lysander and Hermia talk, not of law and duty, but of love and desire. But the contrast in language is not as strong as you might expect, for Hermia uses a legalistic language of her own. Where Egeus and Theseus talked of the laws of Athens, she speaks of *tale* and *history*. Look closely, though, and there is a lot in common between her language (lines 152–157) and the two men's:

> If then true lovers ever have been crossed
> It stands as an edict in destiny.
> Then let us teach our trial patience,
> Because it is a customary cross ...

LEGAL NICETIES

Words like *edict* and *trial* here are legalistic, while *customary* suggests the legal notion of "precedent" – things have always been done this way before, so they should be done the same way now. Hermia is proposing a separate code of law especially for young people, following the precedents laid down by the old love stories and the great lovers of history. ✪ Look at the oath she takes (lines 171–181) – normally we swear by God or by some sacred object like the Bible; what does it say about Hermia's state of mind that she is swearing by these particular things?

BEYOND THE LAW

If the law of Athens forbids their love, Hermia and Lysander decide, they will get out of the city to where the law cannot follow them. Helena appears, feeling that life is all very unfair. Demetrius's love for Hermia, she says, breaks the laws not just of Athens but of common sense. She, Helena, is just as beautiful as Hermia, so why should Demetrius not love her? But love is not logical like this, of course; it is a matter of perception.

Helena says she wishes she could be *translated* (line 195). She cannot be turned into Hermia, of course, but what she is saying may not be quite as absurd as it seems. Love does have the power to change things. Look at Hermia's own comment (lines 207–212) that for her Lysander has turned Athens from a paradise into a hell. Love isn't necessarily all sweet and nice.

37

BEYOND REASON

Love has certainly changed Helena, apparently robbing her of all reason. From the point of view of sheer calculation, it would be in her own interests to cover up for her friends' elopement; that way, Hermia would be out of the picture, and Demetrius might feel he had to settle for Helena after all. Instead, for the hope of a few words of gratitude from Demetrius, she will risk not only her friendship with Hermia, but her own chances of happiness. It makes no sense.

Love breaks the rules, therefore, and throws everything into a different light. Such a different light, indeed, that perhaps it is better suited to darkness, where the things of everyday life cannot be seen and the imagination can range free.

Lysander and Hermia have agreed to meet in the middle of the woods in the middle of the night. There, outside the city, away from the authority of parents and the law, they will find freedom. There, in the peace of the woods, as the night comes down and everyday realities dissolve into darkness, the lovers will be able to imagine their own new world. Anything is possible in the world of dreams.

SPOTLIGHT ON CHANGE

Think about the idea of change. We have seen how the feelings we have can change the way we look at things. As Helena says:

> Things base and vile, holding no quantity,
> Love can transpose to form and dignity.
> Love looks not with the eyes, but with the mind
> And therefore is winged Cupid painted blind.

But the feelings we have can themselves be changed by poetry, claims Egeus. Look at it from his point of view – a bit of moonlight, a bit of mood music, and above all, a bit of poetry, and his dutiful daughter Hermia has been changed into a teenage rebel:

Thou, thou, Lysander, thou hast given her rhymes,
And interchanged love tokens with my child.
Thou hast by moonlight at her window sung
With feigning voice verses of feigning love …
With cunning hast thou filched my daughter's heart …

It may not be quite the sort of wizardry Egeus thinks it is, but words and settings really do have the power to change the way people feel. At its most benign, perhaps this magic might be worked by a love poem like Lysander's. More disturbingly, perhaps it might be a political speech. The person who has command over language may well end up having command over people.

Over to you

? The diagram below shows the command structure of the characters in this scene (who's supposed to obey whom). Try tracing on top of this the love lines (who wants whom). Consider how the two diagrams compare. Can you see any accidents waiting to happen, any conflicts in store?

Theseus   Hippolyta

Egeus

Lysander   Demetrius   Helena   Hermia

? Courtship – what do we know about the courtship of (a) Theseus and Hippolyta (lines 124–128), and (b) Lysander and Hermia (lines 130–137)? Which lady seems to have more choice in the matter, and why?

? How does Helena characterize love in her speech at the end of the scene? To Egeus (line 28) love is a spell. Find three further definitions in the course of the scene.

? What kind of mood do you think Shakespeare creates in this opening scene? Is this to be a light, upbeat play or a dark, downbeat one?

? Divide a sheet of paper down the middle, head one side "Up" and the other "Down," then read through Theseus's opening speech noting in the appropriate column any words that seem to you to suggest one mood or the other. Words that suggest joy, life, light, or indeed, anything positive will belong in the "Up" column; words with darker, more negative associations will go under "Down." Continue through the rest of the scene, and when you've finished, see how the two lists compare.

now that you've seen the nobles, take a break before seeing how the other half lives

Act 1 *scene* 2

◆ A group of Athenian tradesmen plan a performance for the royal wedding celebrations.
◆ They agree to meet the next night to rehearse in the woods outside the city.

☀ The difference in mood in this scene is enormous – light comedy after the drama of the first – but the difference in social tone is perhaps even greater. If, in scene 1 we met some of Athens' higher society, this scene introduces some of the city's workingmen. The difference is clear from the start; you get a strong message from the very names of these men: "Snug," "Snout," and, of course, "Bottom" – comically short, simple, crudely English words next to the elaborate, elegant, classical-sounding names of the last scene: "Demetrius," "Lysander," "Hippolyta," and so on.

CLOTHES AND CLASS

The social difference would be obvious in the men's costumes, of course, and in their gestures and their way of carrying themselves. The minute they entered the stage, it would be clear that they came from a very different class than the aristocrats we have just been watching.

Once they open their mouths, the difference is even more obvious. We saw at the end of act 1, scene 1 how the command of language could lead to the command of people. The opposite certainly seems to hold true: Lack of linguistic command tends to go along with powerlessness. For all their verbal energy, the inarticulacy of the workmen renders their low status unmistakable. To be inarticulate is, effectively, to lack a voice.

The tradesmen's lack of education is clearly comic, but they are not in the play just for us to laugh at. They also serve to point out the pretensions of the more upper-class characters. Bottom doesn't know the story of *Pyramus and Thisbe*, although it is part of classical mythology; if he were more educated, he would. Ignorant as he is, though, he has seen enough bad theater to ask: *What is Pyramus? A lover or a tyrant?* He knows from experience that the lead male character in a play is likely to fall into one of those two categories. In scene 1 we admired Lysander's romantic eloquence and Theseus's regal authority. It does something to the way we regard them to be reminded now that the lover and the tyrant are "stock" characters. Such standard, often-repeated, and thus instantly familiar figures are a convenient shortcut for the busy commercial dramatist, fitting easily into an unfolding action without any need for careful character development.

The disadvantage of such characters is that they are too familiar and too superficially conceived to be either interesting as sketches of human nature or compelling as characters. There is more to both Theseus and Lysander than that, of course, but as readers/watchers we get a more critical take on them when we are reminded that there are conventions – even clichés – in these things. Neither is really a "stock" character, but at the same time, perhaps, both are less special than they themselves like to think.

 SPOTLIGHT ON THEATER

❂ How do you think this group of characters would behave on the stage, *physically*? How would they move, place themselves? Think of a class of seven-year-olds, whose teacher is handing out the parts for the annual school play:

there is always one child who has to be the star, others who shrink back from the prospect of performing, and since a part has to be found for everyone, someone has to play a tree or other piece of scenery!

Funny as this scene is, it has serious things to say about the play as a whole, even, perhaps, about theater more generally. The tradesmen's failure to understand the conventions of theater is obvious; considered more closely, that failure can be seen to spring from two separate misconceptions.

First, there is the view of the stagestruck Bottom. He sees the play as an opportunity for self-exhibition, a vehicle for his own majestic (he imagines) talents. The thought that it might have a wider purpose, in representing a story, creating an illusion, doesn't occur to him.

Until, that is, he is shocked out of his self-regard by Quince: *And you should do it too terribly you would fright the Duchess and the ladies that they would shriek, and that were enough to hang us all.* And that is the second misconception: It is ridiculous, of course, to think that some pantomime lion is really going to frighten anyone. Quince is going to the other extreme and exaggerating the realism of the illusion.

That is the tricky thing about the theater: We believe and we don't believe at the same time. If we are not prepared to let ourselves be fooled at all, we cannot respond to the situations and feelings being represented before us, but we never believe that what's happening on stage is literally "true."

There is magic in the theater. A group of actors have already been transformed into Athenian aristocrats and workmen before our very eyes. It takes imagination, however – Shakespeare's, the actors', and our own.

Try this

? Why do the workmen decide to rehearse their play in the woods?

? Who seems to be the leader of the workmen in this scene? Who is the biggest show-off in the company?

Who would you say was the most timid? Find
something in the text to support your view in
each case.

? This second scene features uneducated men who set
out to say one thing and end up saying another. Look
at how Quince (lines 6–7) seems stupidly to be
contradicting himself (*wedding day at night*) when
really, if you think about it for a moment, what he is
saying makes perfect sense; it is simply awkwardly
expressed. Now go through the scene and write down
all the words you can find that are misused. How do
these mistakes affect what their speakers are trying to
say?

Take a break now – next stop fairyland!

Act 2 *scene* 1

◆ Robin, jester to the Fairy King Oberon, warns a fairy servant
to Queen Titania of his master's rage over the queen's
"theft" of a boy companion.

◆ The royal couple meet and quarrel.

◆ Oberon plots revenge and sends Robin off for a magic herb.
This will make the sleeping Titania fall in love with the first
thing she sees on waking.

◆ Oberon sees a youth (Demetrius) being followed by a
desperate maiden (Helena). He sends Robin after them, so
the magic can be worked on the unfeeling young man
as well.

We are now well into the play, beginning the second act. It
still feels fresh, though, since every scene so far has presented
us with a change in pace and tone (the drop down the social
ladder we saw between act 1, scene 1 and act 1, scene 2, for
instance, and the switch from verse to prose that helped to
signal it) and a new and completely different set of characters:
the young nobles in act 1, scene 1, the *mechanicals* in act 1,
scene 2. This scene, too, introduces a new set of characters,
only this time they are not mortals, but spirits. Notice the

short-lined, rather formal verse these first fairy speakers use, another thing we have not had before (unless you want to count Bottom's "lofty" rhyme in act 1, scene 2, lines 29–36!).

NIGHTTIME IN THE WOODS

We are also in another setting: the woods at night. This difference is one you have to keep consciously in mind when reading the play: in the theater, of course, the very different sort of lighting – dark, shadowy, mysterious – you would have for this scene would make it impossible to miss. Now we really are in a dreamworld, a world of fantasy. The fairy's opening speech suggests a world in which ordinary human rules do not apply. What would be obstacles to us – *bush ... briar ... flood ... fire* – cannot impede this spirit. *Swifter than the moon's sphere*, she travels; the comparison suggests not only speed, but vast, astronomical distances, effortlessly covered.

Everything is extravagantly transformed in this dreamland; the flowers become *pensioners* – a royal bodyguard, laden with rich jewelry. But this image, for all its dazzling beauty, also carries a hint of menace. The queen's guards are, after all, armed soldiers sworn to kill or die in her defense.

THE WILD SIDE

And she might need them to. Look at Robin's speech (lines 18–32). The king may be here to hold *revels*, but he is nevertheless *passing fell and wrath*, and *jealous*. And while the queen may pamper and caress her *lovely boy, so sweet a changeling*, with *joy*, there is a suggestion of violence, too, about the fact that she has *stol'n* him, and now *perforce withholds* him. The elves have to *hide* for *fear*, we are told. There is a world of pleasure and enchantment in the woods, but there are hints too of something more threatening. Groves, greens, and fountains sound enticing enough, but what about *forests wild* (line 25)?

A MATTER OF SCALE

Notice that, in addition to all the other differences in tone and setting we mentioned above, there is a difference in scale. The queen has little flowers for guardsmen, we have already been told, while the frightened elves hide in *acorn cups* (lines 31–32). It is not just a *difference* in scale, though, but a confusion – as we saw in the fairy's opening speech, these tiny spirits take vast distances in their stride, while the queen, we are told, has as a companion, a boy, apparently a human-scale boy from a mortal Indian king. It is hard for us to make sense of these apparent contradictions, but then it is hard to make sense of fairydom altogether – that is the whole point. How, for instance, are we going to pin down Robin when, as the fairy has told us (line 41), he has at least two other distinct identities, as *Hobgoblin* and *Sweet Puck*?

Indeed, both the fairy's remarks about Robin (lines 33–43) and Robin's own proud boasts after that (lines 44–60) suggest that upsetting the normal human routines and ways of understanding things is a large part of what fairydom's activities are about. We see the same when Oberon accuses Titania of manipulating Theseus's behavior for her own ends (lines 79–83):

> *Didst thou not lead him through the glimmering night*
> *From Perigouna whom he ravishèd,*
> *And make him with fair Aigles break his faith,*
> *With Ariadne and Antiopa?*

These represent direct and damaging interventions by the Fairy Queen in the lives of innocent mortal women.

A ROYAL ROW

As Theseus and Hippolyta prepare for their wedding, it is sobering to find Fairyland's royal marriage on the rocks, but then, the spirit realm is, it seems, anything but idealistic. With all the magic powers at his command, there is something sadistic about Robin's love of practical jokes. As for Oberon and Titania, far from being particularly spiritual and regal, it is funny that they are in some ways the most "human" couple in the play; they squabble like any mortal couple (lines 61–65).

Titania's speech (lines 84–120) develops further the association of love with disruption and violence, and gives still greater emphasis to the parallel between dreamworld and reality. The falling out of the fairy king and queen has had disastrous consequences for the mortal world, she says. Their love has always made that world go around; so now, she says, their quarrels have left everything out of joint, even the seasons, the most important rhythm of human life.

Oberon's story about Cupid and his dart adds still another example of the violent, predatory nature love can often assume, and the way in which it can upset the normal order of things. But the magical properties Cupid's arrow left the plant with remind us of another property of love. Squeezed onto a person's eye, the magic herb alters his or her perception of things completely. In that respect, it can stand for love itself. As we said in our discussion of act 1, scene 1, above, love has the capacity to change the way we see.

POINTS OF VIEW

For the moment, though, Demetrius and Helena see things very differently. Demetrius cannot see why she is unable to see the obvious: He simply does not love her. It is no use explaining, and the result is confusion, and transformation, for the desperate Helena willingly imagines herself changed into his *spaniel* (line 210). Her situation, she feels, changes "the story" itself:

> Apollo flies, and Daphne holds the chase.
> The dove pursues the griffin; the mild hind
> Makes speed to catch the tiger: bootless speed,
> When cowardice pursues, and valour flies.
>   (lines 238–241)

The confusion Helena describes is comparable to the disorder described by Titania earlier, but Helena's hunting image has associations of violence and destruction too. For all the terrible natural disasters described earlier in the scene, the mood has not really started to darken until now. Demetrius's warning (lines

?   In lines 161–180, Oberon describes how Cupid's arrow fell on a flower. How did it change that flower's appearance? And how did it change its properties – what magical powers did it give the flower?

?   Just about everybody who is anybody in this scene is either watching or following somebody else. Below is a list of the main characters in this scene. Join the names in sequence to show who's watching/following whom. Start with the audience, ourselves. After all, we're watching everybody else:

Audience

Helena

Oberon

Hermia and Lysander

Demetrius

if you want to stay more alert than Titania does in the next scene, take a break

---

Act 2 *scene* 2

- ◆ The fairies sing to Titania.
- ◆ As Titania sleeps, Oberon squeezes juice from the herb onto her eye.
- ◆ Lysander and Hermia arrive, lost and exhausted. They lie down to sleep until daylight, lying chastely apart, as they are still unmarried.
- ◆ Robin mistakes them for the couple his master sent him after, and treats Lysander with the herb.
- ◆ Helena arrives, Demetrius having finally managed to shake off her pursuit.
- ◆ She wakes Lysander, who promptly falls for her.
- ◆ Helena assumes it's a sick joke, and runs off, but lovesick Lysander follows.
- ◆ Hermia wakes up abandoned and alone.

For all the magic charms the fairy song is supposed to contain, it casts its most effective spell not as a piece of supernatural sorcery, but as more earthly, artistic enchantment, as a soothing lullaby, which puts Titania to sleep in seconds. The everyday magic of music casts the strongest spell of all. The combined effects of melody and harmony, the regular rhythms of the fairies' verses, and the stately spectacle of the dance are so strong that the song casts a soothing spell over Titania, even though the tone of its lyrics is actually anything but calming, raising ideas of "creepy-crawlies," even poisonous snakes. So if Titania is soothed, we as the audience are not. We sense that the sinister side of Oberon's *I know a bank …* speech (act 2, scene 1, lines 256–275) is echoed in the song's words, even if its rhythms and music recall the more pleasurable side of Oberon's speech.

HELENA'S TRANSFORMATIONS

Helena feels Demetrius's rejection has transformed her: she is *as ugly as a bear*, she says (line 100); her love's rejection has in some sense turned her into a *monster* (line 103) from whom *beasts* flee (line 101). Moments later, however, she undergoes a second ironic transformation. Remember Helena's wish (act 1, scene 1, line 195) to be *translated* into Hermia? Well, with Hermia's supposed love, Lysander, suddenly in love with *her* instead, it is almost as if she had been!

ALL TALK

Lysander in his poetic mode can sometimes seem too eloquent by far. It is not his fault, of course – he has been bewitched – but there is something disturbing, nevertheless, in the way Lysander can declare his passionate poetic love to two different women in as many minutes. The language of love is supposed to be the most intimate, heartfelt sort of speech. Ironically, though, we find that the same words do just as well whatever woman is being wooed. ❍ How likeable a character do you now find Lysander?

Hermia is left alone in the woods. Within this dreamworld, she has had a dream of her own, and it has not been a pleasant one. The serpent mentioned in Oberon's *I know a bank …* speech and the fairies' song at the start of this scene (also, perhaps, the monster Helena thought she herself was turning into) has finally turned up in this horrible form. The *knight* (line 151) who should be saving this damsel in distress has instead sworn his allegiance to Helena. There is a real sense of shock and violence about Hermia's speech: *Help me, Lysander, help me!* You can almost feel the *crawling serpent* at her breast, feel her *quake* with fear, see her *swoon*. The attack may be a figment of her imagination, but her response to it is vividly physical.

Your Turn

? Why does the magic herb have to be applied to Titania's eyes, rather than any other place?

? How do Lysander and Hermia come to be lying apart from one another? And how does Robin manage to mistake them for Demetrius and Helena?

? Look back at the diagram you did at the end of act 1, scene 1, p. 39, showing the characters and their love lines. How do things look now? Draw in the new lines in a different color if you want.

next we see that love really is blind — but first, take a break

Act 3 *scene 1*

◆ The tradesmen have gathered in the woods to rehearse their play.

◆ Robin gives Bottom the Weaver an ass's head and the others flee in alarm.

◆ Titania wakes up, sees Bottom, and falls instantly in love.

Once again the workmen ludicrously overestimate the likely realism of their play. Unfamiliar themselves with the conventions of theater, they assume that others will take their acting for reality, and so they devise elaborate strategies for making their play acceptable by undermining its dramatic impact. They fail to understand, also, that there is no need to have actors playing inanimate objects like the moon and the wall. Flute, in line 92 on, will run his whole part together without waiting for the other characters to speak. All in all, in showing how a play should not be staged, this scene does a pretty good job of making us think what a remarkable thing a successful theatrical performance really is.

From line 81, we get our first look at the actual words of the tradesmen's play. Shakespeare may be having fun at the expense of lesser talents than his own, but he is also making a more serious point about poetry and its capacity to shape the way we look at things.

If good poetry can seduce us, bad poetry can turn us off. A tale of two lovers, separated by a wall and by the enmity of their families, it is easy to imagine the story of *Pyramus and Thisbe* being a moving romantic drama, even if here it is quite the reverse. Comedy or tragedy – it's the way you tell it!

STYLE AND LANGUAGE

❂ What do you think of the way the author of *Pyramus and Thisbe* tells it? He is not helped by his actors, of course. Confusing *odorous* with *odious*, and telling Flute that Pyramus has gone off to *see a noise*, Bottom makes clear just how far he is out of his depth intellectually. But even without his ignorant mistakes, how accomplished a piece of writing do you think this is? Pyramus, for example, is *lily white* and *red rose* in consecutive lines. Leaving aside the contradiction, how original do you think these images are?

Thisbe's comparison of her love with a true, tireless horse is picked up comically when Bottom appears with the head of an ass. Robin's speech (*Sometimes a horse I'll be, sometime a hound …*) underlines this idea of transformation, while adding a further note of menace to the proceedings. As we found before, in act 2, scene 1, there can be a vicious quality to Robin's practical jokes, and this threat to harass Bottom's friends in a series of animal forms shows real aggression toward men who have, after all, done him no harm. In fact Bottom is the one who harries them, although unintentionally, when he reenters with his ass's head and they scatter in panic. Their fear and flight at his appearance are especially funny given the fuss they made earlier about how their stage lion might frighten the ladies (lines 27–35).

MAKING AN ASS OF BOTTOM

As Quince now points out, Bottom has been *translated*. This is the same word Helena used (act 1, scene 1, line 195), and it echoes her later feeling (act 2, scene 2, lines 100, 103) that she had been turned into an ugly animal. Although Bottom does not understand what has happened to him, he comes comically close without realizing it when he says *This is to make an ass of me*, though he obviously only means it in the sense of "making a fool of." Oberon, remember (act 2, scene 2, lines 33–40), wanted Titania to wake to love some ferocious animal. By making Titania fall in love with the ass-headed Bottom, Robin is going one better. Titania's loving a fierce animal would just be dangerous and inappropriate; her loving Bottom in this form will be ridiculous and humiliating. In making an ass of Bottom, Robin is making an ass of her.

ASS OR ANGEL?

Titania is awakened by Bottom's singing (his braying voice as different as can be imagined from those of the birds he is singing about!). She thinks he sounds like an angel (line 131); but then she also thinks he is *as wise as* [he is] *beautiful* (line 150)! She is under the spell of Oberon's herb, of course.

Notice that, while the queen speaks in verse here, verse that catches in its rhythms the gentle, romantic mood of Fairyland and love, Bottom speaks in his usual rambling prose.

Added to this, Bottom's perceptions are basic and matter-of-fact, and Titania's exaggeratedly romantic. It is as if they are taking part in different scenes. Titania offers a dreamy existence of *jewels* and *flowers* that recalls the fairy's description of Fairyland at the beginning of act 2, scene 1, and Oberon's *I know a bank* ... speech at the end of that scene. Bottom, however, is speaking crude common sense, and the contrast is comic.

Another comic contrast comes with the arrival of the fairies. From their very names they seem tiny and insubstantial beside Bottom's lumbering bulk. Look at Titania's instructions to them for Bottom's care (*Be kind and courteous to this gentleman* ...). The fairies' lightness and tiny size is repeatedly emphasized.

The scene ends with a grotesque sting in the tail, in Titania's closing remark that her minions should *Tie up my love's tongue; bring him silently*. Bottom's braying conversation is, it seems, making the illusion of his beauty and gentility difficult to maintain, even for Titania in her bewitched state.

 ## SPOTLIGHT ON BOTTOM

Part of the humor in Titania's courtship of Bottom, we have seen, stems from the difference between Titania's attitude of romanticism and Bottom's crude common sense. Another comic aspect, we find, is the ludicrous difference in size between Bottom and his attendants. But the situation is also absurd from the point of view of sex roles and social class as Shakespeare's audience would have seen them. We saw when we looked at act 2, scene 1 that it flies in the face of convention – changes *the story*, as Helena put it then – that the lady should be wooing the gentleman. But it changes the story even more outrageously when, as here, the lady is a queen and the man a common weaver.

Likeably enough, Bottom doesn't know how to behave in the grand role bestowed on him by the queen. He chats pleasantly and on equal terms with the fairies appointed to serve him. Charming as this may be, it would have seemed grossly comic to the play's original audience, marking a preposterous collapse of authority, an absurd reversal of the normal social order.

Got the picture

? The workmen decide they must reassure the female members of their audience on two points. Can you say what they are?

? They also discuss two more technical challenges, things they feel will be hard to represent on stage. What are these, and how do they decide to get around them?

? Pyramus and Thisbe are supposed to meet by moonlight. Which other couples in the play have met by moonlight?

? From their very names, as we said above, the fairies called by Titania (line 164) to look after Bottom seem

tiny and insubstantial. Now look at Titania's more
detailed instructions to them in lines 170–180. Write
down the words and phrases in this speech that
suggest the fairies' airy lightness and miniature scale.

*now that you've gotten to the Bottom of this
scene, take a break*

Act 3 *scene* 2

◆ Robin tells Oberon he has carried out his order, but it
becomes apparent that he has treated the wrong couple.

◆ When Demetrius lies down to sleep, Robin has a second
chance to put things right.

◆ This time Helena arrives. Already being pestered by
Lysander, she now finds Demetrius declaring his love as
well.

◆ Hermia returns, accusing her of stealing Lysander's love,
and Helena concludes that her former friends have joined
up to taunt her.

◆ As the women quarrel, the men go off to fight a duel over
Helena.

◆ Oberon tells Robin to lead the lovers off through the woods
until each has been matched with his or her right partner.

This scene features three ill-matched couples: first, Titania and
Bottom, as described by Robin to his master, Oberon; second,
Hermia and Demetrius; third, Helena and Lysander.

 STYLE AND LANGUAGE

Notice that, just as Robin's magic has given Bottom an
ass's head, his words now give an animal form to the
other mechanicals; they scattered, he says (lines 20–21), like
geese spotting a wildfowler or *choughs* (crows) hearing a gun.

In his wooing of Hermia, from line 45 on, Demetrius is
using the same language of love we have seen Lysander
use. It is wildly inappropriate, not only because of Hermia's
negative feelings toward Demetrius (to whom, remember, her
father has been trying to marry her against her will), but

because of the real distress she's in following her nightmare and abandonment. She fears Lysander is literally dead. But Demetrius has a lover's easy way with words. When Hermia accuses him of murder, he replies that she is murdering him by breaking his heart (lines 60–61), hence Hermia's exasperated exclamation (line 70): *O, once tell true, tell true.* All this flowery, riddling language has left her dizzy. She is desperate for some plain speaking, for someone to tell her genuinely and simply what has happened to someone she genuinely and simply cares about.

The unscrupulousness of love and its language are again highlighted when Lysander offers to *yield* Demetrius his *part* in Hermia, if Demetrius *bequeaths* him his share of Helena's love. Love is now speaking the same language of law and property that Egeus was speaking in act 1, scene 1. Demetrius, too, makes poetic language work for him, saying (lines 174–176) that his heart went to Hermia only as a guest, and that Helena is its true home. The merest play on words, this "argument" still seems to satisfy him.

A FRIENDSHIP ON THE ROCKS?

Believing that her friend has joined with the others to make a fool of her (line 198), Helena recalls the long friendship that once joined her to Hermia. The separation of two such friends (*Two lovely berries moulded on one stem,/… two seeming bodies but one heart*) involves real violence. The distress Helena feels when her wish to be *translated* into her friend is granted, and the shock that results for Hermia herself, illustrate again the darker potential of love. Helena's speech also highlights the damage that the violent passions of love can do to what are in many ways more real, lasting relationships, such as her lifelong friendship with Hermia. We saw at the end of act 1, scene 1 how the lovesick Helena was prepared to betray her friend's elopement for a word of gratitude from Demetrius. Now the women's apparent rivalry in love is poisoning their whole friendship. ❂ How do you rate the relative value of love and friendship? How do you think Shakespeare sees them?

The situation degenerates into farce, Lysander shaking off Hermia's embrace and (lines 270–271) calling her *cat …*

serpent (the last is especially unkind, given the monstrous snake that attacked her in her recent dream). Now it is Hermia's turn to be transformed into an animal. Comparing her to a "burr," a prickly plant part, places her even lower down the evolutionary scale so is perhaps still more insulting. Ridiculous though it may be, this attack still leaves a bad feeling. Bewitched as he is, Lysander doesn't merely prefer Helena, he feels a physical revulsion toward Hermia. She has become something *vile*.

The women, hitherto inseparable friends, are now fighting. Such a violent falling out between two such ladylike characters is a shocking spectacle. There is humor, of course, in hearing Helena deliver a view of Hermia she has apparently revised since her all-but-sisters speech earlier (lines 204–224). Now she recalls that Hermia *was a vixen when she went to school* (line 341).

STYLE AND LANGUAGE

There is humor, too, in seeing how the language the women use in describing one another, especially on the subject of height, matches the descriptions we have been given of them by their poetic male admirers. Demetrius, says Helena (lines 231–232), has just described her as *goddess, nymph, divine, and rare,/ Precious, celestial.* Now (line 311), Hermia calls her a *painted maypole.* Hermia's unflattering description underlines the exaggeration in Demetrius's.

Notice, too, that the height question, a running joke through the rest of the scene, is only introduced because Hermia misinterprets a comment of Helena's. Her word *puppet* (line 303) is obviously intended as an attack on Hermia's integrity, reinforcing the preceding charge that she is a *counterfeit*, a fake, a pretend person. Hermia, however, immediately thinks it's a reference to her size. This is a nice human touch: We are so used to hearing Hermia described in Lysander and Demetrius's extravagant terms that it is a surprise to find that this model of poetic perfection is an ordinary young woman who is sensitive about her height.

THE DARKEST HOUR

But for all the humor, this is the play's bleakest phase by far. By now what we have is a Midsummer Night's Nightmare. We have already talked about the dark, ruthless side of love and the slippery, sinister side to poetic language. We have also seen, especially in Robin's sadistic streak, a less appealing side to the powers of magic and Fairyland. All seems to have come together here to leave a desperate, irredeemable mess.

But if this is the play's darkest moment, a moment, thankfully, is all it is. Oberon's anger with Robin brings us an immediate sense of relief. Normally, anger is a negative emotion; here, however, it is our guarantee that Oberon's intentions are basically good, that he is committed to bringing things to a happy conclusion.

The first thing to be done, says Oberon, is that Demetrius and Lysander, who have gone off into the woods to fight a duel over who is to have Helena, must be separated. The *drooping fog* (line 378) in which they are to lose themselves will, paradoxically, redouble the darkness of night and take them through darkness and confusion to the light, clarity, and understanding of day. In a single line, therefore, we find a hint as to the possible purpose of the play as a whole, a journey through darkness, suffering, and confusion to a better, more enlightened existence. The fact that the fog is to be *as black as Acheron* – one of the rivers of Hades, the Underworld, to which the dead made their way in the myths of classical Greece – suggests that this journey can even be seen as a sort of death and rebirth. All of this makes an outwardly light comedy suddenly seem like a very serious drama indeed!

A NARROW ESCAPE

Robin's speech about the approaching dawn (*My fairy lord, this must be done with haste ...*, lines 399–409), also hints at a much darker side to the supernatural than has mostly been acknowledged so far. In the account of Fairyland at the beginning of act 2, scene 1, for instance, or the world

Titania offers Bottom in act 3, scene 1, line 154 on, Fairyland is associated with gentleness, luxury, light, happiness, and abundance. We have already had inklings at various points that this is not all there is to it. But Robin's description here is by far the most chilling we have had. Think what it would have done to the tone of the scene if it had come before Oberon's words of reassurance! Coming after them, it still sends a shudder down our spines. We feel we have had a narrow escape from forces much too dark for comfort.

But Oberon again (lines 410–415) disassociates himself from this sort of supernatural existence. He is the sort of spirit who can stay up until dawn, he says, meaning that, though on occasion mischievous, he is basically benevolent. His urgings to Robin to *make no delay;/ We may effect this business yet ere day* (lines 416–417) suggest that the action has passed its crisis. All that remains is to sort out the confusion and tie up the loose ends.

Robin's song (lines 418–422) and his actions in leading the two would-be duelists astray echo his gloating words in act 3, scene 1, lines 107–113 (*I'll follow you, I'll lead you about a round …*) and his cruel taunting of the mechanicals once Bottom has been transformed. This time, though, the action is kind, another sign that what has been wrong in the night's activities is now to be made right.

The whole unhappy mess, says Robin, when Hermia appears in an anxious state, indicates that:

Cupid is a knavish lad
Thus to make poor females mad.

This is too much, given his own contribution to the upset and confusion, but now, he says, anointing Lysander's eyes to restore his love for Hermia, everything is going to turn out all right:

Jack shall have Jill,
Naught shall go ill,
The man shall have his mare again,
And all shall be well.

STYLE AND LANGUAGE

The simple names and plain, nursery-rhyme form of this little verse show up the elaborate artificiality of the sort of poetic love language we saw the aristocratic young lovers using earlier in the scene. It makes a bit of a joke of love, making something blunt and awkward of an emotion that has previously been described in rather grander, more elegant terms, but there is no harm in that. We have seen throughout that the elaborately poetic terms in which Lysander, in particular, has described love can be misleading and unreliable. We have seen, too, that love can be a violent, changeable, and disruptive thing. It is important, therefore, to remember that it is also a basic fact of human existence; that is what Robin's words remind us of, in their homespun, even

 vulgar simplicity: In all times, at every level of society, young men and women have paired off into loving couples.

Test yourself

? In the quarrel between Helena and Hermia in this scene, the former's height and the latter's shortness become a sort of running joke, with even Lysander eventually joining in. Look through the scene again from line 296 to line 365 and note down the different words and phrases in which the idea recurs.

? Look closely at Robin's speech (lines 399–409). What sort of picture of the supernatural world does it present? Which words and phrases help give this impression? Now look back at the fairy's speech in act 2, scene 1, lines 8–17, and see how the language of the two speeches compares.

*now that a happy ending is in sight,
take a break*

Act 4 *scene* 1

◆ Oberon releases Titania from her spell and they are reconciled.

◆ He gives Bottom his own head back, and leaves him sleeping.

◆ Theseus, Hippolyta, and Egeus arrive for a dawn hunt. They find the young people sleeping, now perfectly matched in love, Demetrius with Helena, and Lysander with Hermia.

◆ Egeus is angry, but Demetrius says he is happy with the way things have turned out. Theseus rules that the lovers should all be married in the same ceremony as he and Hippolyta.

◆ Bottom wakes up, astonished, and rushes off to tell the story of his amazing dream.

As we saw at the end of the last scene, the real drama is over. Now that Oberon has undertaken to make things come out all right, we have no real doubt about the eventual outcome, but if the action is almost finished, what are the next two acts of the play supposed to be for? Some sense must be made of what has happened, for both characters and audience. Not necessarily rational common sense, but emotional, poetic sense. That is what the last two acts will be about.

TITANIA'S LOVE NEST

The scene opens in an atmosphere of obvious eroticism, with Titania's invitation to Bottom to sit down with her on a *flow'ry bed* (line 1), while she heaps caresses on him. But it is hard to take such a seductive mood seriously, given Titania's references (lines 2–4) to her lover's *amiable cheeks*, his *sleek smooth head*, and *fair large ears*! ✪ How do you think the actors playing Titania and Bottom should play this scene?

✪ As in act 3, scene 1, there are absurdities of scale here; how far do you think one bag's worth of honey would go for a full-grown man? And it is hard to imagine a man like Bottom having such delicate appetites. Look what happens when the queen calls for music; somehow, you can't help thinking that *the tongs and the bones* (lines 29–30) probably were not on the whole what she had in mind. Once again, as we saw

61

earlier, at the end of act 3, scene 1, Bottom's crudeness contrasts with the delicacy and refinement of Fairyland.

There is a lot of humor here about Bottom's peculiar state, in between humanity and asshood, the man being surprised to find his face so *marvels hairy* (line 25) but the ass in him craving oats, hay, and dried peas (lines 32–35, 38–39). The main contrast, though, is between the heavy grossness of humanity in general and the lightness and sophistication of fairydom; thus, the squirrel's nuts Titania offers Bottom sound like fairy fare, found in the woods themselves. The things he is asking for, on the other hand, sound like something from the farm, but Titania returns to the woods for the images she uses to suggest their embrace (lines 43–46):

> *So doth the woodbine the sweet honeysuckle*
> *Gently entwist; the female ivy so*
> *Enrings the barky fingers of the elm.*

Notice how the subject word *woodbine* and its verb *entwist* are placed on either side of the object word *honeysuckle*, as if it really is "entwisting" it.

HAS OBERON'S TRICK BACKFIRED?

It is no wonder, therefore, that Oberon should find the scene disagreeable when he comes upon it. We may find it charming, although comic; to him it is neither. His view of Bottom (line 50) as a *hateful fool* seems unjust, given the weaver's complete innocence in this whole affair and the part the king himself played in bringing it about. Could he be a little jealous, seeing his wife like this – even of the ass-headed Bottom? This was all Oberon's own doing, of course, his big scheme to punish and humiliate Titania, but he is the one who has ended up feeling punished and humiliated to see his wife in bed with an ass.

The ups and downs of human affairs are, we were told earlier in Titania's big speech at act 2, scene 1, lines 84–120, influenced by the changing moods of the immortals. Now Oberon's softening attitude toward Titania signals a coming restoration of normality in the human world.

STYLE AND LANGUAGE

By line 64, Oberon is using the word *hateful* to describe the *imperfection* caused to Titania's eyes by the magic herb he placed on them. When this speech began, he was applying the word *hateful* to Bottom. The drift of this adjective from the one object to the other is revealing, reflecting as it does Oberon's movement from an irrationally angry blaming of the innocent Bottom to a realization that what has happened has been the result of his own foolish trick.

Oberon calls Titania *my queen* again (line 89) when he invites her to dance with him. Their dance seals their reconciliation and anticipates the dancing there will be at Theseus's and Hippolyta's wedding feast the following night, at which the temporary confusion of the play's mortal lovers will be resolved in marriage.

As in act 2, scene 2, music accompanies the working of magic; again, it has access to feelings that words cannot reach. The regular rhythms of these short, mostly rhymed lines (89–106) emphasize the stability of the emotional order now prevailing in the play.

The idea of music, therefore, links this section with the following one, the arrival of the royal hunting party being heralded by the sounds of horns, and Theseus commenting in line 110 on the *music* of his hounds. In fact, the word *music* at this point stands for something rather different, suggesting not order and stability, but profound disorientation. The *musical confusion/ Of hounds and echo in conjunction* (lines 114–115) resembles the crazy chaos of the sound track in a modern science fiction or fantasy film at the moment where the action crosses a border of time, space, or some other dimension, and we move with the characters from one state of reality to another. Hippolyta's recollection of her hunt with Heracles and Cadmus has the same effect:

> *Never did I hear*
> *Such gallant chiding; for besides the groves,*
> *The skies, the fountains, every region near*
> *Seemed all one mutual cry.*

The whole scene seems to dissolve into sound here, heralding the lovers' emergence from their magic sleep.

The huntsmen's horns sound, and the lovers are suddenly back in the daytime world. Though geographically we are still in the woods, in the world of magic and of night, we are effectively back in everyday Athens, where Theseus, not Oberon, is ruler.

Athenian law exists here, and under that law Egeus has rights over Hermia and over Lysander, who, in legal terms, is her abductor. But Demetrius disagrees and, under the law, Theseus, as duke, can overrule Egeus, and the law of romance, coinciding with the good of Athens, may be allowed to prevail.

Left behind by the departing hunting party, the lovers wonder what has happened to them. Hermia's sense is that she is seeing things *with parted eye,/ When everything seems double*. The idea recalls the theme of perception that has played such an important part in the play. How you see things determines how they are; thus, with her eyes treated with the magic herb, Titania was able to see Bottom with the ass's head and find him beautiful. Hermia here is seeing double, which is actually appropriate enough. Right now she has a foot in both worlds, she feels, the magical night world and the cold light of day, and she cannot be sure which of the two actually represents reality. As Demetrius puts it:

It seems to me
That yet we sleep, we dream. Do not you think
The Duke was here, and bade us follow him?

He is talking about Theseus's appearance, as if *he*, the solid, businesslike Duke of Athens, were a dreamy, insubstantial spirit. It takes Demetrius and his friends several moments to decide that: *Why then, we are awake …*

COMPARING NOTES

Demetrius's parting remark that *by the way let us recount our dreams* (line 209) reminds us that, although for the audience it has been a collective entertainment, Demetrius, Lysander, Hermia, and Helena have each experienced the night's marvels individually and in a certain sense alone. They did not actually share the same experience, thus the need now to fill one another in. They have to work over the night's events and try to establish what has happened because, while each has been caught up in his or her own personalized "dream," each has awakened in some significant sense changed by what has happened.

Demetrius's dream has ended with his ardently wooing the girl he earlier spurned, while Lysander, after for a time vehemently spurning the girl he loved, now has the official permission to marry the one he never thought he would get. Hermia was abandoned for a time in the heart of the woods, while Helena, who had to tag along behind the rest, unwanted by anyone, before her strange if temporary transformation into everybody's love, now finds herself, after this strangest of nights, with the one love she really wanted all along. What has happened, while less solid than reality, has clearly been more substantial than a dream. If it is a dream, it is a dream whose effects have persisted past waking.

HOME TO ATHENS

As we said at the start of act 1, scene 1, the daytime world is the only one we are really at home in; we cannot live permanently in the world of dreams, enticing as that might (in some ways) seem. But while it is important for the young lovers that they now return to daytime Athens, we still feel that, without their night of difficulties, they would have missed out on something important. The things they have seen and felt may have been figments of the imagination, but their legacy has been real enough. The bonds the lovers have formed as a result of their night in the woods are now unbreakable; their everyday Athenian reality has been touched by beauty, by enchantment.

This, of course, is one of the things art can do for us, one of the things that we may take away from our experience of A Midsummer Night's Dream. Viewed at face value, the play is the merest fiction, a dress-up game for grown-ups who ought to know better. Somehow, we sense, though, that it is something more than that. Unreal, insubstantial, but by no means untrue or empty, the experience of a theatrical performance has a very tangible effect on our lives, the imaginary influencing our reality. That feeling of wonder, of magic, of the extraordinary that we find not only in plays but in music, books, films, and other works of the imagination enhances our appreciation of the ordinary here and now.

Test your recall

? The loving togetherness of Titania and Bottom in the first part of this scene obviously annoys Oberon. What words and phrases show his displeasure, in lines 47–71?

? Demetrius's final choice of a love has been altered by his experiences in the woods. In trying to explain this change of heart from line 167 on, he uses a couple of images of natural transformation. Can you find them in the text?

? What are Theseus's plans for the four young lovers as he leads them out of the woods (lines 184–193)?

? There have been many references to music in this scene, especially (lines 110–132) with the idea that the sounds made by a pack of hunting dogs is itself a kind of music. Look back at this section and see if you can find words in the text that suggest what kind of music this is.

now Take a break before the wedding preparations begin

Act 4 *scene* 2

◆ The mechanicals are upset at Bottom's transformation – and the failure of their play.

◆ Bottom arrives, safe and sound. He has wonders to reveal, he says, but it will have to wait, since their play has been chosen for performance at the royal wedding celebrations.

Most obvious here is the difference in perspective between the working people of Athens and the play's more aristocratic characters. His friends' admiration and affection for Bottom is clear, but as poor men they cannot help feeling the financial loss involved in his disappearance. As Snug says, *If our sport had gone forward we had all been made men,* "made" in the sense of being made, set up, for life. The difference in perspective is further underlined by Snug's mention of the *two or three lords and ladies more* to be married. It comes as a bit of a shock to us, having become so involved in the stories of Lysander and Hermia and Demetrius and Helena, but to Athens' lower classes they are, of course, very distant, anonymous figures.

Bottom's advice to his friends about their performance is, once again, amusingly literal-minded. Thisbe must have clean linen, and the lion not cut his fingernails, or what will he do for claws? Most of all, however, the actors must keep their breath free of onion or garlic. That way it will be sweet, and if their breath is sweet, he concludes – with crazy logic – their comedy will be too.

THREE WORLDS

As an audience, or as readers, we have seen the different characters in the play up to now as participants in a collective, shared experience. As we saw previously (act 4, scene 1, line 209), though, that is not quite how they themselves have experienced it.

A Midsummer Night's Dream is not just about a collection of individuals; it contains three different classes whose lives have been separate, except for colliding at certain crucial points. At the top of this hierarchy is (1) the world of Oberon and Titania – Fairyland. Below that is the mortal world, which naturally seems to subdivide itself: (2) the aristocratic class that contains Theseus, Hippolyta, Egeus, and the young lovers, which seems so far removed from (3) the class comprised of the *mechanicals* that they might as well be in different worlds.

We have already seen how the fallout from Oberon and Titania's marital disputes has affected events in the human world. We have seen it affecting the young lovers who happened to stray into the woods on a night when Oberon was there with magic on his mind. Worlds 1 and 3 have seriously collided only once, in Titania's ludicrous love for the transformed Bottom. But it is an interesting comment on the social order within the play that, as of the end of act 4, worlds 2 and 3 have yet to meet at all. Bottom, Quince, and company might have been in a different play altogether from Theseus, Hippolyta, and the young lovers, for all the contact they have had up to now.

Take a break before the grand finale

Act 5 *scene* 1

◆ The next evening, Theseus and Hippolyta discuss the events of the night before.

◆ Egeus announces the entertainments to be offered. Theseus chooses *Pyramus and Thisbe*.

◆ The play is a shambles, but still good-naturedly received.

◆ Theseus brings the celebrations to a close and the mortals go off to bed.

◆ Oberon, Titania, and Robin bless the house and the newlywed couples.

This scene finds us back in Athens, the dreams of the past night now firmly in the past. As far as Theseus is concerned, indeed, they never even happened, for he is profoundly skeptical about the lovers' story. *The lunatic, the lover and the poet*, he says, *Are of imagination all compact.* Within the world of the play, we know, he is wrong: These marvels really did take place.

For us, however, his words have their implications. The three categories share a tendency to project the contents of their fantasy onto the world. The lunatic, in his delusions, peoples his world with demons; the lover thinks his beloved beautiful, however hideous the reality; the poet weaves whole worlds out of *airy nothing*, as of course the author of *A Midsummer Night's Dream* has done. *Such tricks hath strong imagination*, argues Theseus:

> *That if it would but apprehend some joy*
> *It comprehends the bringer of that joy;*
> *Or in the night, imagining some fear,*
> *How easy is a bush supposed a bear.*
>   (lines 20–23)

If we let the imagination have its way, says Theseus, we let our wishes and fears color our view of reality. But can any of us really avoid doing this, every day of our lives? Theseus's rationalism is, when you think about it, every bit as distorting, blinding him as it does to what we know – within the world of the play, at least – has truly taken place.

 ## STYLE AND LANGUAGE

We have seen how, for much of the play, the aristocrats in the cast have tended to speak in verse, the lower-class workmen in prose. Here this tendency is reversed, the prose comments of the duke and his friends throwing into relief the actors' unaccustomed verse-speaking. And it is unaccustomed – notice how mixed up Quince gets in his prologue, confused as he is between line ends and sentence breaks.

Whatever illusion there may be in this play-within-the-play is stretched to the limits by its audience's little observations throughout, but is of course completely shattered when Bottom, hearing Theseus's observation in lines 194–195, breaks off to set him straight (line 196). The illusion keeps being suspended during this performance; it will be deliberately broken in Snug's speech as gentle lion (lines 232–240), in the interests of reassuring the ladies in the audience, and collapse through sheer vexation later (lines 271–274) when Starveling, tired of trying to deliver his lines above his audience's relentless heckling, lapses into exasperated prose.

Once again, these players' failure to understand the conventions of theater make us think a little harder about how those conventions work for us. Theseus sums it up (lines 224–226) when Hippolyta dismisses the whole show as silly: *The best in this kind are but shadows, and the worst are no worse if imagination amend them.* The audience's imagination is having to work overtime to "amend" matters here, of course, but Theseus is right – no play can hope to do without it completely, not even one of Shakespeare's!

The play ended, Theseus sends the lovers off to bed, an order that creates a strict demarcation between day and night. We said before that it was significant that Theseus had taken no part in the central, nighttime woods section of the play. Now, he says, midnight has struck; it is *almost fairy time*. Given his comments at the start of this scene, it seems likely that this is a joking remark. Having seen the play unfolding, however, we know it is truer than he realizes.

ROBIN HAS THE LAST WORD

As if on cue, Robin appears, his speech, like his earlier one in act 3, scene 2, lines 399–409, laying emphasis on the negative side of night (how different his lion is to Snug's, for example), but reminding the audience that there are good fairies, too, who will see that all in Theseus's house are kept safe from harm. For a speech of reassurance, it is a little strange. While it is nice to know that the fairies are going to be providing protection, is it not unsettling to be reminded as vividly as this of the terrors they are going to be protecting the household *from*? Oberon's speech, too, with its references to the kind of disfigurements that *could* afflict the couples' children, is as disturbing as it is soothing. ✪ How would you edit it to make it more reassuring?

The main point is, however, that the action will conclude with its gaze fixed firmly on the future. Life will go on holding its fears and its dangers, but it *will* go on; that is the main thing. This closing scene has been an opening scene as well, bringing together every category of character who has appeared in the play – court, commoners, and immortals alike – to celebrate a grand collective marriage and therefore the start of a new generation.

In describing the spirits as *shadows*, Robin's closing speech echoes the remarks Theseus makes earlier in the scene (line 224) about the theatrical illusion (*The best in this kind are but shadows …*). As he goes on, Robin blurs the distinction between night and day, weaving together ever more closely the idea of theater, enchantment, and dreams:

Think but this, and all is mended:
That you have but slumbered here,
While these visions did appear;

His remark about the *serpent's tongue* – an audience's hiss of disapproval – seems to bring us out of the dream and return us to the theater, where a play has just finished; yet the image also reminds us of the serpent that shed its skin on Titania's bank (act 2, scene 1, line 263), the one that attacked Hermia in her dream-within-the-dream (act 2, scene 2, lines 152–156), and the various other serpents who slide menacingly through the play and its imagery. If we give Robin a good hand in applause, though, it is as if we are offering him a hand to shake in friendship, and therefore sealing the deal we have made in accepting the truth of his play.

Your Turn

? Bottom's speech, lines 179–193, is obviously terrible, but why exactly? Look at it more closely: What effects was the author of *Pyramus and Thisbe* trying to achieve here, and where did it all go wrong? How about his speech in lines 287–302 when he finds the mantle? And Flute's, as Thisbe (lines 341–364): Why does this seem so ridiculously untragic? Think about line lengths, rhyme, rhythm, and the use of particular words. (Look especially at the comparisons this speech gives for Pyramus's features. How appropriate do you think they are?)

Topics for Discussion and Brainstorming

One of the best ways to review is with one or more friends. Even if you're with someone who hardly knows the play you're studying, you'll find that having to explain things to your friend will help you to organize your own thoughts and memorize key points. If you're with someone who has studied the play, you'll find that the things you can't remember are different from the things your friend can't remember, so you'll be able to help each other.

Discussion will also help you to develop interesting new ideas that perhaps neither of you would have had alone. Use a **brainstorming** approach to tackle any of the topics listed below. Allow yourself to share whatever ideas come into your head, however meaningless they seem. This will get you thinking creatively.

Whether alone or with a friend, use Mind Mapping (see p. vi) to help you brainstorm and organize your ideas. If you are with a friend, use a large sheet of paper and colored pens.

TOPICS

1 Now that you know *A Midsummer Night's Dream* so well, how about rewriting it? You (and a friend) could try retelling the story of the play from the point of view of one of its characters. That isn't as easy as it sounds. Remember, not everyone shares the same experience. Theseus never goes into the nighttime woods, for instance. Also, as a duke, whom everybody has to look up to, he has a very different perspective from that of a young girl like Hermia, who has to (or at least who is supposed to) just do as she is told. Lysander and Quince both have their own very different way with words; how might each describe the *Pyramus and Thisbe* performance in act 5, scene 1? And how would Bottom's perspective on things compare with that of a more educated character like Demetrius? Or a less innocent one like Robin? Find lines in the text to support your view of what their view would be. Choose a character and try it now.

2 How do the different social groups in *A Midsummer Night's Dream* differ from each other, reflect each other, and perceive each other?

3 Discuss how authority is presented in *A Midsummer Night's Dream*.

4 What transformations take place in *A Midsummer Night's Dream*, and how are they significant?

5 How are the different settings important in *A Midsummer Night's Dream*?

6 What aspects of love can you identify in the play? Use the illustration on p. 74 to help you.

7 How many different verse forms can you find in the play? What reasons can you see for the variations? In Shakespeare's blank verse, can you find lines that depart from the rigid (iambic pentameter) norm? In each case, why do you think Shakespeare has done this?

8 What part does humor play? Is the clownish comedy just there for "light relief," or does it tell us something more serious about human life?

9 The moon is an important image in *A Midsummer Night's Dream*. Because the old moon gradually grew fat, then produced a tiny new one, the ancients associated it with pregnancy, birth, and death; its dazzling whiteness, on the other hand, made them think of maiden chastity. These paradoxical qualities can both be found in *A Midsummer Night's Dream*, as can the sheer sense of atmosphere that moonlight creates. Trace the image of the moon through the play; what roles do you see it playing?

10 What different things does magic mean in *A Midsummer Night's Dream*?

11 For immortals, Oberon and Robin are particularly prone to what we call "human error." Why might this be, and what do you think it tells us?

12 Think about the different roles that men and women have in the play. Do you see any patterns emerging? Who's in charge, and who does Shakespeare think should be?

Any of these topics could appear on an exam, but even if you think you've found one on your actual exam, be sure to answer the precise question given.

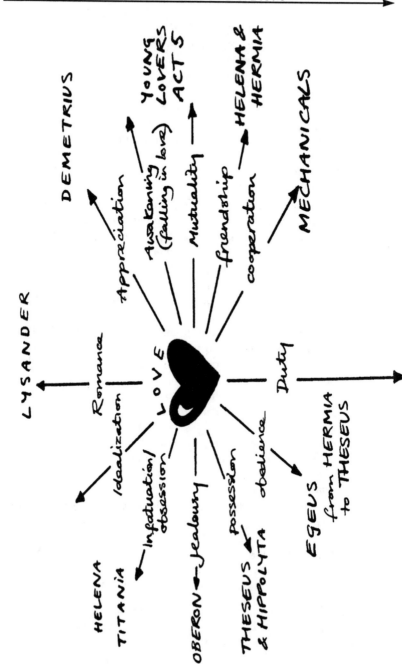

LYSANDER

DEMETRIUS

YOUNG LOVERS ACTS

HELENA & HERMIA

MECHANICALS

Appreciation

Awakening (falling in love)

Mutuality

Friendship

cooperation

Romance

LOVE

Duty

Idealization

Infatuation/obsession

Jealousy

possession

obedience

from HERMIA to THESEUS

HELENA

TITANIA

OBERON

THESEUS & HIPPOLYTA

EGEUS

74

In all your study, in coursework, and in exams, be aware of the following:

- **Characterization** – the characters and how we know about them (what they say and do, how the author describes them), their relationships, and how they develop.
- **Plot and structure** – what happens and how it is organized into parts or episodes.
- **Setting and atmosphere** – the changing scene and how it reflects the story (for example, the use of the city of Athens and the woods to reflect reality and dream).
- **Style and language** – the author's choice of words, and literary devices such as imagery, and how these reflect the mood.
- **Viewpoint** – how the story is told (for example, through an imaginary narrator, or in the third person but through the eyes of one character – "She was furious – how dare he!").
- **Social and historical context** – influences on the author (see Background in this guide).

Develop your ability to:

- Relate **detail** to **broader content, meaning, and style**.
- Show understanding of the author's **intentions, technique, and meaning** (brief and appropriate comparisons with other works by the same author will earn credit).
- Give a **personal response and interpretation**, backed up by **examples** and short **quotations**. (Use short, appropriate quotations as "evidence" of your understanding of that part of the text. Don't just put down large chunks for the sake of it.)
- **Evaluate** the author's achievement (how far does the author succeed and why?)
- Use literary terms to show your understanding of what the author is trying to achieve with language.

THE EXAM ESSAY

Planning

Writing an excellent essay on a theme from *A Midsummer Night's Dream* will challenge your essay writing skills, so it is important to spend some time to plan your essay carefully.

1   Make a **Mind Map** of your ideas on the theme suggested. Brainstorm and write down any ideas that pop into your head.
2   Taking ideas from your Mind Map, **organize** them into an outline choosing a logical sequence of informaiton. Choose significant details and quotations to support your main thesis.
3   Be sure you have both a strong **opening paragraph** stating your main idea and giving the title and author of the literary work you will be discussing, and a **conclusion** that sums up your main points.

You could remember this as the **MOG** technique.

Model answer and essay plan

The next (and final) chapter consists of a model answer to an exam question on *A Midsummer Night's Dream*, together with the Mind Map and essay plan used to write it. Don't be discouraged if you don't think you could write an essay up to this standard yet. You'll develop your skills if you work at them. Even if you're reading this the night before your exam, you can easily memorize the MOG technique in order to do your personal best.

The model answer and essay plan are good examples for you to follow, but don't try to learn them by heart. It's better to pay close attention to the wording of the question you choose to answer on the exam, and allow Mind Mapping to help you to think creatively.

Before reading the answer, you might like to do a plan of your own, then compare it with the example. The numbered points, with comments at the end, show why it's a good answer.

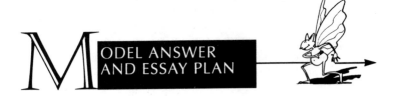

MODEL ANSWER AND ESSAY PLAN

In some works of literature the author chooses to depict worlds and characters very different from our own. Explain how Shakespeare's *A Midsummer Night's Dream* presents us with the intertwining of a fantastical fairy world, of which Titania is the

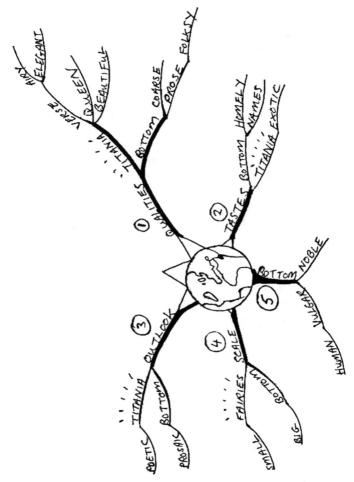

queen, and the more mundane world of the citizens of Athens, who include both aristocrats and the working class.

PLAN

1 Thesis statement; title, author, and setting of literary work to be discussed.
2 Setting of the play in more detail – Athens, the wild woods; the fairy world as opposed to the real world; the inhabitants of each.
3 Bottom as a symbol of the coarse, the ordinary, and the homely; his language and tastes.
4 Titania as a symbol of the fairy world – the exotic and sophisticated; her language and view of the world.
5 The contrast between the two characters and their purpose in the play highlighting the differences between the real and the fantastical.

ESSAY

Authors of many works of literature invite their audience into imaginary worlds quite different from our own. These fantasy places may be other planets, as in much science fiction, or utopias set in distant places. Shakespeare, in his comedy *A Midsummer Night's Dream*, chooses to introduce his audience to both ancient Athens and to Fairyland. Human Athenian society resembles our own, with a variety of characters both highborn and lowborn, but the inhabitants of Fairyland and their queen are very different.

The play opens in the court of Athens where Duke Theseus and Hippolyta are to be married and the "hempen homespuns," a group of laborers, are to give a little play or entertainment celebrating the wedding. In the human world we are also introduced to four young lovers – Helena, Hermia, Lysander, and Demetrius, whose misadventures in love lead them into the woods where the worlds of the human and the fairy intertwine. The other main setting of the play, the woods, far away from ordinary life, are inhabited by the fairies who are ruled over by Oberon and Titania. These fairies are presented as diminutive in size and capable of traveling great distances in the wink of an eye.

Bottom the Weaver is the leader of the group of Athenian workers who have traveled into the woods, the realm of the fairies, to rehearse their play. He is a comic character, full of his own importance, who mostly speaks in earthy prose in contrast to the smooth regular verse of Titania, the Fairy Queen. Even his name, "Bottom," is plain and unromantic. Because Robin, that master of mischief, has anointed Titania's eyes with a magic herb, when she wakes from sleep she falls in love with the first thing or person she sees – and that person just happens to be Bottom wearing an ass's head. This is one of the most comic scenes in the play because of the great contrast between the Fairy Queen and her most unsuitable earthly beloved. "What angel wakes me from my flow'ry bed?" The very unangelic Bottom answers:

> *The finch, the sparrow and the lark,*
> *The plain-song cuckoo gray,*
> *Whose note full many a man doth mark,*
> *And dares not answer nay.*

He remarks on such commonplace birds and uses plain language, where Titania says:

> *Mine ear is much enamored of thy note;*
> *So is my eye enthralled to thy shape.*

and uses much more sophisticated and elevated language. When Titania declares: "Thou art as wise as thou art beautiful," Bottom replies, in typical fashion: "Not so, neither."

If clumsy Bottom is seen as a symbol of the earthly and has problems explaining his play to his co-workers, Titania may be seen as magical and powerful as she orders her minute fairies, Peaseblossom, Cobweb, and Moth, to "gambol" in Bottom's eyes. Everything about her is otherworldly, lovely, and light as when she asks her fairies to "pluck the wings from painted butterflies/ To fan the moonbeams from his sleeping eyes."

Shakespeare uses the interaction between Titania and Bottom to contrast the mortal and immortal worlds in *A Midsummer*

Night's Dream. His imagined world of the fairy realm is indeed a world that is very different from our own. In Fairyland, the most improbable things happen and magic and spells abound. In this wonderful comedy of love, where all is righted in the end, Shakespeare has indeed created a delightful imaginary place.

WHAT'S SO GOOD ABOUT IT?

1 Opens with strong thesis statement.
2 Gives title, author, and setting of literary work to be considered.
3 Introduces different types of characters in the play.
4 Gives a clear explanation of who Titania and Bottom are.
5 Clearly explains their different uses of language.
6 Employs specific quotations from the play's text.
7 Is written in clear, accurate, standard English.
8 Concludes with a summary proving the thesis statement.

OTHER ESSAY THEMES FROM A MIDSUMMER NIGHT'S DREAM

Other themes you may want to consider when writing an essay on the play might include:

1 Love is a very popular theme in literature. As Lysander says in *A Midsummer Night's Dream*, "The course of true love never did run smooth . . . ." Show how this is true for the main characters in the play.
2 Discuss the use of magic and enchantment in Shakespeare's *A Midsummer Night's Dream*.
3 *A Midsummer Night's Dream* is filled with images drawn from the natural world, especially animals, birds, and plants. Explain how Shakespeare uses these images to enhance the audience's enjoyment of the play.
4 Robin Goodfellow, also known as Puck, declares: "Lord, what fools these mortals be!" Which characters do you consider to be the most foolish? Explain with reference to the plot of Shakespeare's *A Midsummer Night's Dream*.

GLOSSARY OF LITERARY TERMS

alliteration   repetition of a sound at the beginnings of words, for example, *The raging rocks/And shivering shocks* (act 1, scene 2, lines 29–30).

aside   a short speech spoken by one character, as if thinking aloud; not meant to be heard by others onstage.

blank verse   the kind of nonrhyming verse in which Shakespeare usually wrote, with five pairs of syllables to a line, with the stress always on the second syllable; unrhymed iambic pentameter (see p. xii).

context   the social and historical influences on the author.

couplet   *see* **rhyming couplet**.

dramatic irony   *see* **irony (dramatic)**.

foreshadowing   an indirect warning of things to come, often through imagery.

iambic pentameter   verse with five pairs of syllables to a line, with the stress always on the second syllable.

image   a word picture used to make an idea come alive; for example, a **metaphor**, **simile**, or **personification** (see separate entries).

imagery   the kind of word picture used to make an idea come alive.

irony   **(dramatic)** where at least one character onstage is unaware of an important fact that the audience knows about, and that is somehow hinted at; **(simple)** where characters say the opposite of what they really think, or pretend to be ignorant of the true facts, usually to show scorn or ridicule.

metaphor   a description of a thing as if it were something essentially different but also in some way similar; for example, . . . *we must starve our sight/From lovers' food* (act 1, scene 1, lines 227–228).

personification a description of something abstract as if it were a person; for example, . . . *angry winter* (act 2, scene 1, line 115).

prose language in which, unlike verse, there is no set number of syllables in a line, and no rhyming.

pun a use of a word with two meanings, or of two similar-sounding words, where both meanings are appropriate in different ways.

rhetoric the art of effective or persuasive speaking or writing.

rhyming couplet a pair of rhyming lines, often used at the end of a speech.

setting the place in which the action occurs, usually affecting the atmosphere; for example, Athens, or the woods.

simile a comparison of two things that are different in most ways but similar in one important way; for example, *So we grew together,/Like to a double cherry* (act 3, scene 2, lines 213–214).

soliloquy a speech spoken by an actor alone onstage as if thinking aloud.

structure how the plot is organized.

theme an idea explored by an author; for example, perception.

tragedy a play focusing on a tragic hero or couple (for example, *Pyramus and Thisbe*).

tragic hero a character whose nobility or achievement we admire, and whose downfall and death through a weakness or error, coupled with fate, arouses our sympathy.

viewpoint how the story is told; for example, through action, or in discussion between minor characters.

INDEX

Ⲭ